KATHY HALBREICH

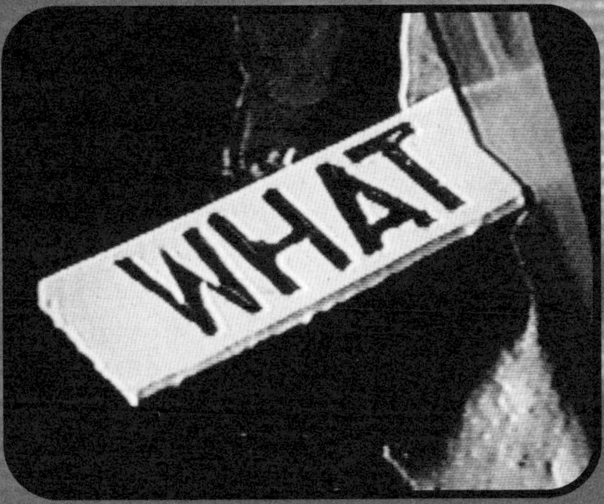

DO YOU

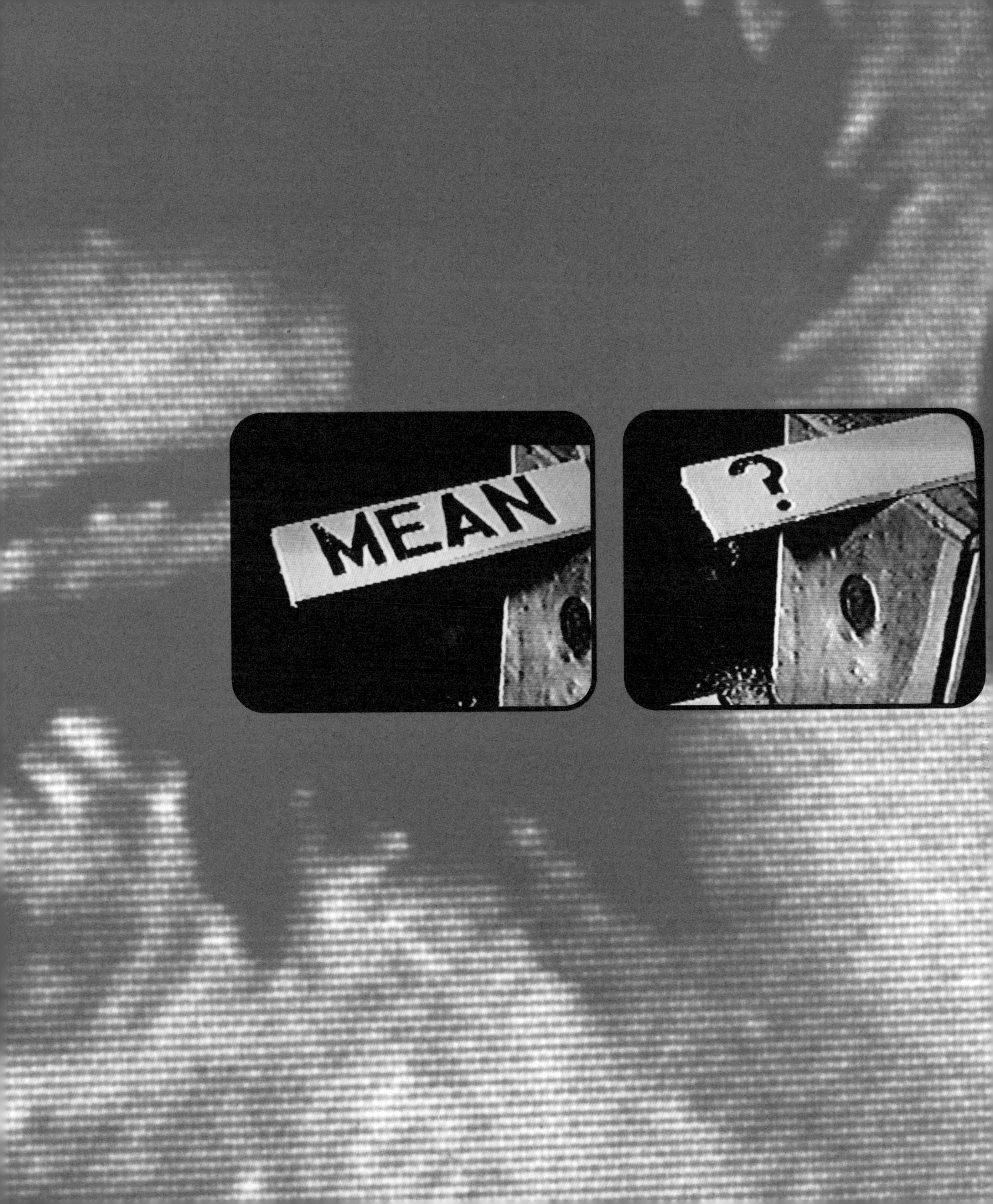
MEAN
?

FOR DAN,

With thanks to KWR.

ELLEN ROTHENBERG

Johanna Branson, editor

Library of Congress Cataloging-in-Publication Data
Ellen Rothenberg/Johanna Branson, editor; contributors, Johanna Branson,
Whitney Chadwick, Lynne Cooke, Daniel Eisenberg, Cindi Katz.
80 p. 21 x 25 cm.
Includes bibliographical references.
ISBN 1-880593-02-5 $17.50
1. Rothenberg, Ellen, 1949– — Criticism and interpretation.
2. Installations (Art) — United States. 3. Conceptual art — Untied States.
I. Rothenberg, Ellen 1949– . II. Branson, Johanna. III. Chadwick, Whitney.
IV. Cooke, Lynne. V. Eisenberg, Daniel. VI. Katz, Cindi.
N6537.R628E42 1994
709'.2— dc20 94-11124
CIP

Distributed by D.A.P., Distributed Art Publishers
636 Broadway, Suite 1208 New York, NY 10012
1-800-338-2665, Fax: 212-637-2887

Editor: Johanna Branson

This book on the work of Ellen Rothenberg documents the artist at mid-career. Four essays concerning different aspects of her work frame the reproductions; arranged according to medium, and roughly chronologically, the images document the artist's explorations into a range of creative expression. Papermaking, performance, object making and installation have occupied Rothenberg throughout her 16-year career.

While the materials and the vehicular approach often differ, much of Rothenberg's work springs from a singular approach to art making. Fabricated or found objects and images, often made of commonplace materials, engage the viewer's own everyday experience, triggering a rich set of associations. The resulting amalgam of shared or public visual materials and private responses finally floats in one's consciousness like a memory or dream, firmly connected to one's experience yet still somehow outside of it.

A sense of Rothenberg the person/artist beautifully emerges from Johanna Branson's interview in which history, motivation and influences are brought forward. Branson, who teaches art history at the Massachusetts College of Art, helped shape the book both conceptually in early discussions with the artist and practically as editor of the publication. Filmmaker, writer and teacher Daniel Eisenberg explores the ways in which Rothenberg articulates the political through formal means, how content is made visual. Space — and how Rothenberg makes and breaks boundaries — is the subject of Cindi Katz's essay. Katz, a cultural geographer involved in environmental psychology and feminist social theory, comes at Rothenberg's work from an unusual angle at the intersection of geography, history and identity. Lynne Cooke, an art historian and curator, connects Rothenberg's aesthetic with her artistic behavior; the artwork is driven not solely by the senses but by history, memory and truth. Art historian Whitney Chadwick describes Rothenberg's most recent work, the three installations comprising the Anne Frank series. She relates the artist's interest in the nature of history, documents and archives to how identity is constructed.

Rothenberg's site-specific installation for Tufts Art Gallery, *The Conditions for Growth*, is the third piece from the Anne Frank series. Rothenberg has gathered a variety of objects and materials in an evocation of a warehouse where things are labeled and stored, in hiding, waiting for interaction — measured, classified and categorized, like the life of Anne Frank. Rothenberg provokes us to consider the talented and curious adolescent revealed in Anne Frank's unexpurgated writings and to ponder the process of history and the ways in which she has been obscured by subsequent "editions" of her life.

A forest of thermometers bound to rulers on strings eerily defines a space through which viewers are encouraged to move and take full measure of themselves with pencil marks on the gallery walls. Can we ever meet the expectations others hold for us? Glass display cases on dollies, placed randomly in the gallery, further the warehouse metaphor. In one such case, white kid gloves, laden with associations of gender and class, are pierced through each finger with safety pins. This pointed reminder of the cool remove of gloved hands is underscored in another pair with ink on the fingertips. Rothenberg likens the myth of Anne Frank to the girl with gloves, quiet and demure. That myth leaves no room for Anne writing about her sexuality and anger at her mother. The gloves also address moral responsibility, action and inaction. When does one "take the gloves off?" In another pair, gashes are sutured with red embroidery thread, evoking both vulnerability and healing strength.

This staging of multiple associations runs through all of Rothenberg's work. She situates encoded materials in various contexts and allows their meaning to unfold in a beautiful and strangely rhythmic fashion. Rothenberg's installation at Tufts has afforded me the pleasure of experiencing this contextualizing process, a process in which the artist connects seemingly simple materials and objects in moving ways. I have enjoyed seeing the artist at work and coming to know her warmth and humanity.

Support for *The Conditions for Growth* was provided by the New England Foundation for the Arts with additional funds from the National Endowment for the Arts and the Massachusetts Cultural Council. A grant from the Tides Foundation provided the initial impetus for a monograph on Rothenberg. Further funds from the LEF Foundation permitted the book to move forward.

Many thanks to the triad who worked so hard to give birth to the publication: Ellen Rothenberg, Johanna Branson and Judy Kohn, whose considerable and inspired talent is evident in the design of the book. I would also like to acknowledge the insight of the essayists Whitney Chadwick, Lynne Cooke, Daniel Eisenberg and Cindi Katz, each of whom took a different but targeted path into Rothenberg's aesthetic, provoking thoughtful interaction with her work. Many thanks to Lois Rimassa and Domtar Specialty Fine Papers for their support. Thanks also to Frederick Kalil, Joanna Soltan and the entire staff of Tufts Art Gallery for their supportive roles in bringing the book to fruition.

Elizabeth Wylie
Director, Tufts Art Gallery
February 1994

Figure 1: *The Great Circle*, performance, 1987
Central Square,
Cambridge, Massachusetts

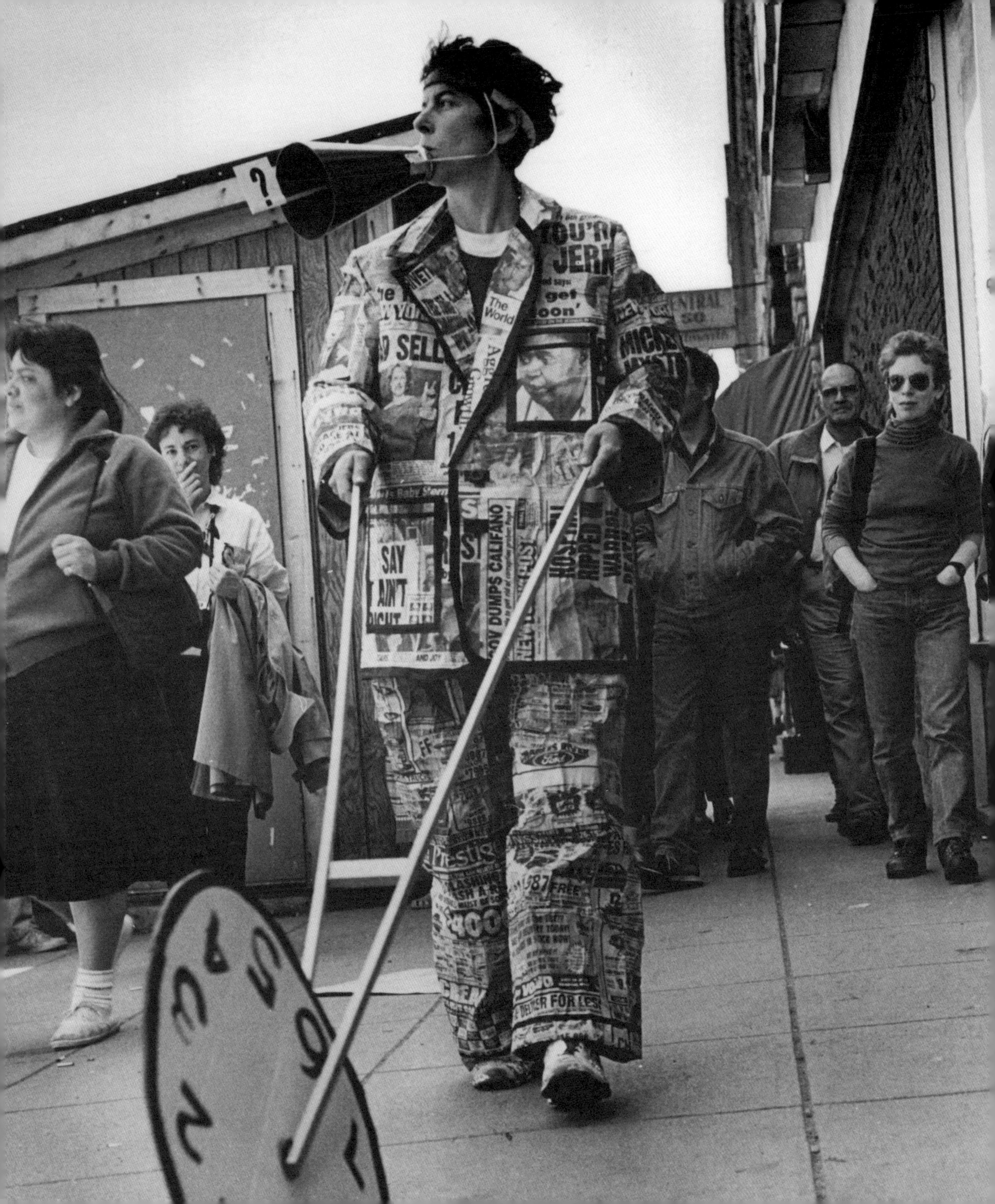

?
JERK
The World
SAY
AIN'T
GOV DUMPS CALIFANO
CENTRAL
SQ.
Prestige

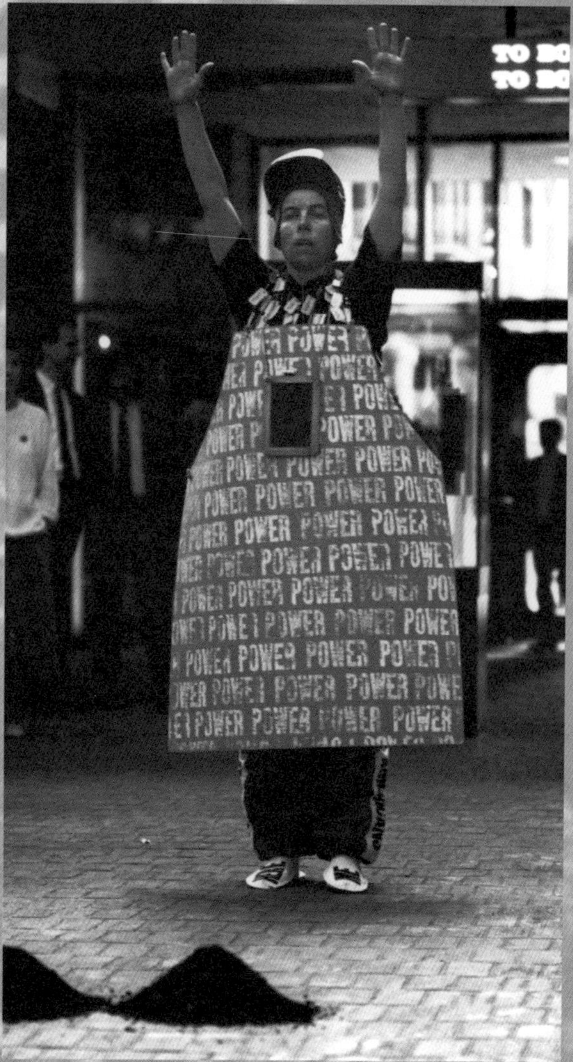

Figure 2 (above):
Common Sense,
performance, 1988
City Place Atrium,
Boston, Massachusetts

Figure 3 (background):
Common Sense, detail

Figure 4 (right):
Plant Man, 1988
photo collaboration with
Bruce T. Martin

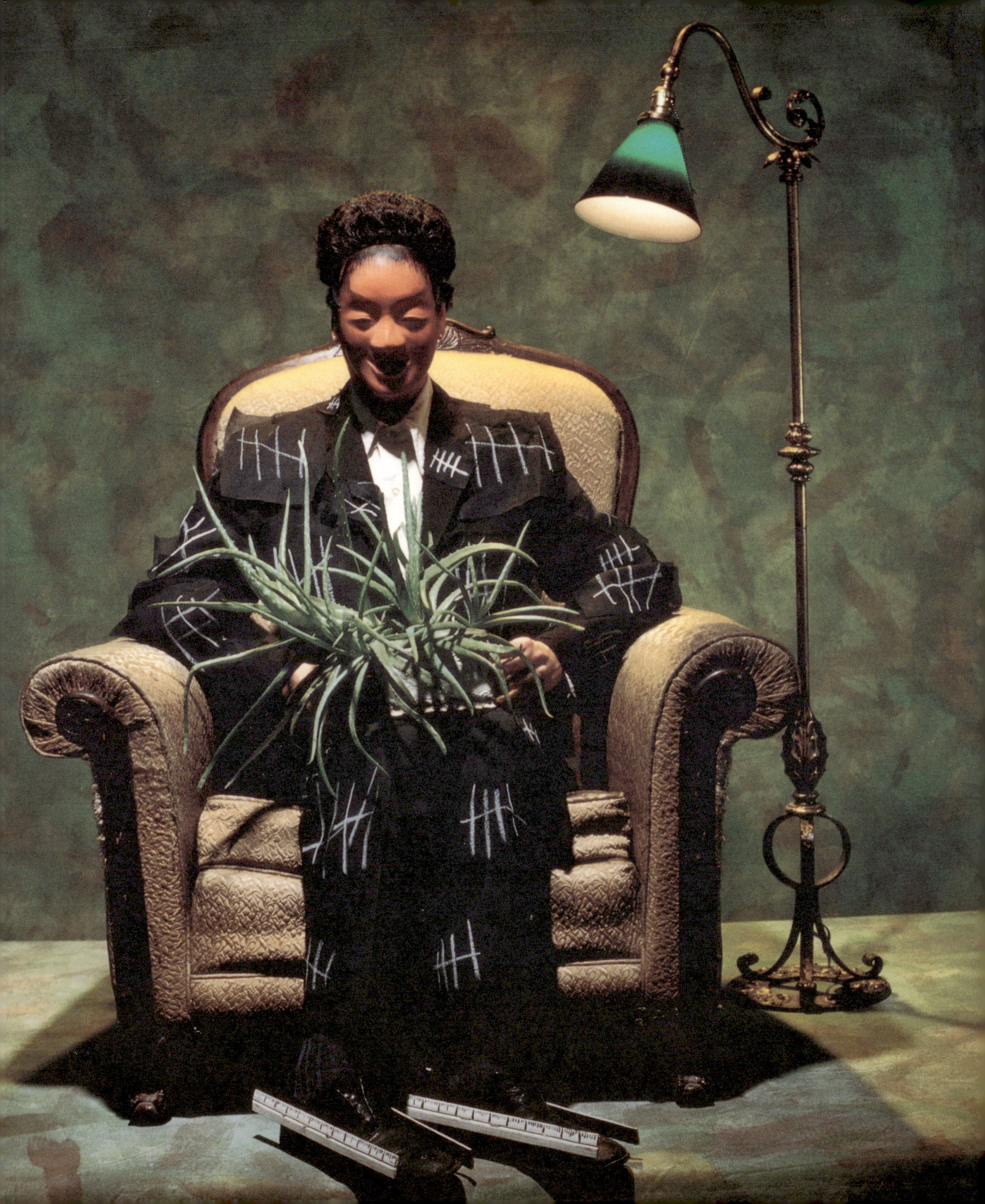

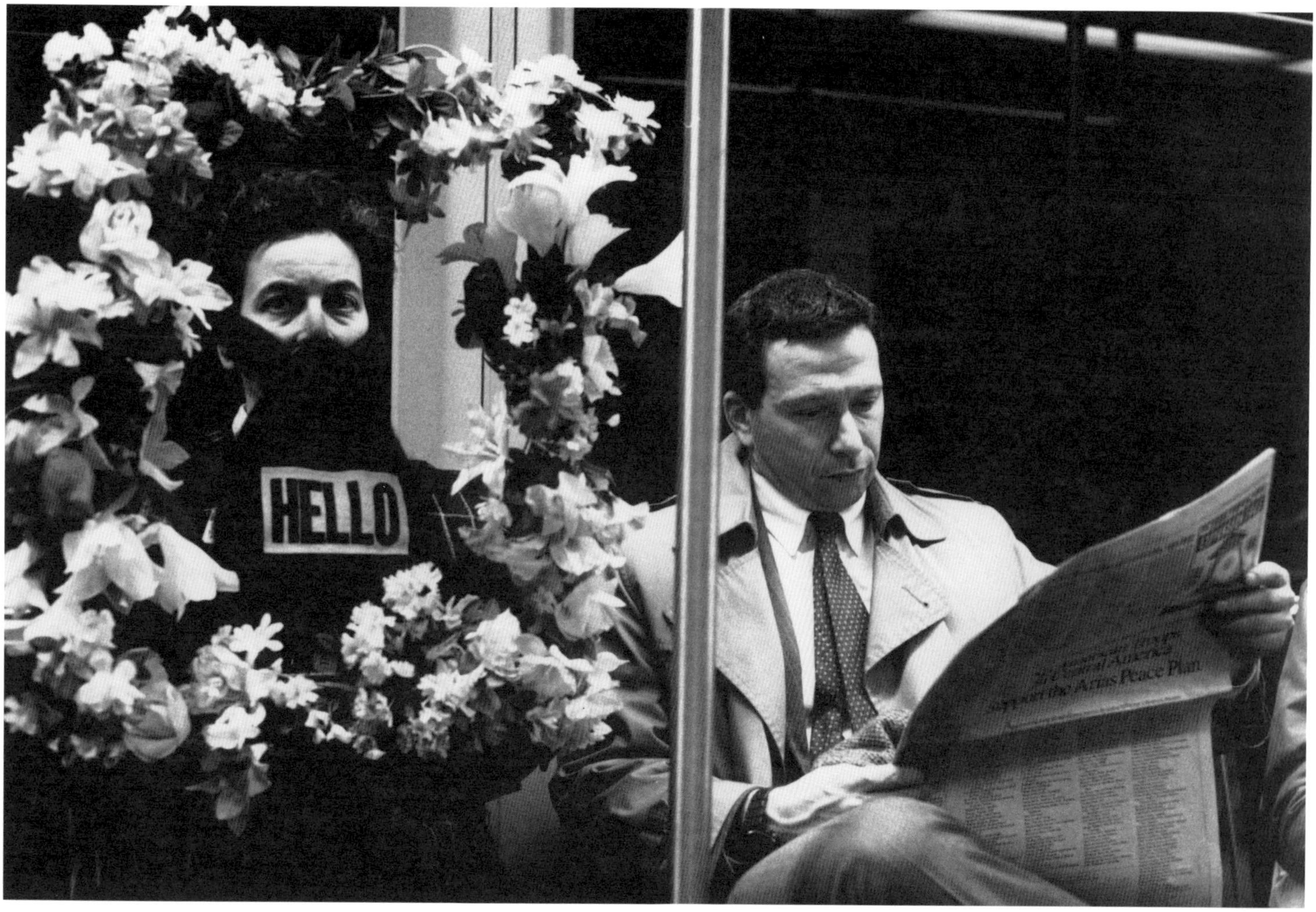

Figure 5: *Subway Rebus*,
performance 1988
Massachusetts Bay Transit Authority,
Red Line

Interview with Ellen Rothenberg

BY JOHANNA BRANSON

JOHANNA BRANSON: I perceive a similar structure in most of your work, from the early performances to recent installations, in which the viewer is asked or obliged to participate in the construction of meaning. Do you see this as being true?

ELLEN ROTHENBERG: I have an interest in making work that resists a singular or static reading, work that operates on different levels simultaneously, that requires a re-viewing or a re-visiting by the viewer. Often, the intellectual or conceptual center is outside the individual pieces which make up a larger work. Meaning is rarely resolved within a single object, a single action or a single image, but derives instead from an additive associative resonance. This is a non-specific, non-linear relationship that can be reconfigured in different combinations. Meaning is formulated by a cumulative reading of the work.

On the surface the works in performance, on paper and in installation seem dissimilar, although the central ideas in the work cross disciplines. I'm not presenting conclusions and I'm not presenting finished arguments; I'm asking questions. Often there are loose ends and a certain level of ambiguity. The form asks the viewer to construct meaning out of fragments, and to respond to the questions in the work, perhaps with a question of his or her own. In that sense, the work demands participation. In *The Great Circle* (Fig.1) and *Subway Rebus* (Fig.5) — two performance pieces, one which took place in the city streets and the other in the subway system — many people actually travelled from location to location with the work. There was a similar fragmentation in *The Marginal Way* (Fig.34), an installation which was located throughout the architectural framework of two two-story structures. There were no maps; viewers encountered the installation sites in the same way that they might discover something on the street. Without an itinerary, the viewer's own experience would be pulled into the work, and the viewer would be asked to construct meaning out of all of these parts, and make some decisions about their relationships. There wasn't a prescribed meaning.

JB: Do you think it's accurate to say that earlier in your work, you personified this searching, or thinking, or mulling over things, that in your performances you were a kind of protagonist?

ER: I became involved in performance because there was certain subject matter — ideas, and experiences — that I wanted to discuss but I didn't have the language to do so. Somehow it was necessary to insert myself in the work. It became an immediate, transformative experience.

JB: Could you be more specific about this subject matter?

ER: Sexual identity, homelessness and the difficulties of economic survival, the boundaries of social relationships. I was preoccupied with the question, "Where should art be located and who is the audience?" Performance allowed me to puncture the distance that exists between the act of making art and the audience and it gave me a voice and an arena for physical action. By moving outside of arts institutions to public sites for performance, I was able to broaden the audience for the work.

However, after a number of years of performing a contradiction emerged; the dilemma of being situated within the work did not allow me any perspective. It was impossible to have a contemplative relationship to what to what I was doing.

JB: I'm struck by what you said about turning to performance as a way of draining out the distance between you and the audience. In the installations and the other kinds of work that you are doing now, it seems to me that you still accomplish that. Do you think that's in any way as a result of the materials that you use?. I guess what came to mind as you were speaking was your use of everyday materials and your personalization of them, whether it's belts or shoes. Sometimes I think your use of mundane, shared materials also punctures the distance between you and the audience.

ER: I've never thought about materials functioning in that way. Perhaps the use of common objects draws the viewer into the work through his or her associations or particular history with these objects. I feel like I've always been drawn to certain objects, for example pencils and erasers. As a child, pencil cases and fresh notebooks of paper were extremely powerful objects. Going to the stationary store before the year started to purchase these things was a ritual act that suggested the promise and potential of the year. I've carried that sense of the object — its life, the object's innate power, its use — to the objects I make or have fabricated. I have a preference for objects that have a certain material integrity. Where the materials of the object are not disguised but refer to the process of its making.

JB: Can you give an example?

ER: Tools attract me. As a child, my family visited historical reconstructions like Sturbridge Village. The exhibits are explanations of how life was lived and how things were made —for example, candle making or spinning. Often there were people in costume demonstrating the task or process. The explicated process, the evidence of the hand, and the clarity of how things worked was comprehensible, even to me as a child. There was nothing hidden or unavailable. The tools themselves were hand-made and their form revealed how they worked. The sense of the hand, of activity, is important. I am interested in objects and materials which may not be in common currency but suggest a certain history. They might reference an outdated technological process or the historical period during which they were used. For example, I prefer letter press printing and find that the pressing of the metal letter into the paper has its own beauty and distinct quality that computer generated type doesn't have. And I'm interested in the fabrication of objects, so I work with people who do casting or metal construction and whose shops and technology are more from the 19th century or early 20th century than the late 20th century.

JB: Why that time period? You're talking about a world of objects that was disappearing after our grandparents' generation. Is there any particular reason that it's that generation of materials?

ER: Maybe it's the last kind of technology that I can understand. Often it requires some hand labor, and most of them are made from machines that are not electronic.

JB: That are still based on hand movement.

ER: Hand movement and the role of the body is central in my attraction to both materials and objects. Some of my choices grow out of my experience as a performer, where the body and physical activities are at the center of the work. Those are fundamental connections. For example, I find I'm attracted to shoes: to the activity of walking, the ability to transform yourself by putting on other peoples' shoes, to insert yourself in "their shoes."

JB: There's a clear connection in the objects between the materials and how they were made physically. You can understand them. In a way, they're repositories of knowledge. And they encourage you to continue to think about the associations of the time in which they were made. They always have implications for direct action as well.

ER: And use. The reason that the work draws people in is because people project themselves within it. People's associations with the particular materials and the suggestion for use inherent in the objects, makes a connection with the viewer. People can look at the belts in *Das Wesentliche* (Fig.40) and say it's about abuse. It's about beating. It's about bondage. It's about the body. It's about corseting. Printing a text describing skin on skin. It's about a visceral connection. I have my own associations and reasons, but I want to hook into other people's experience.

JB: It's clear that gender and sexual identity have been important issues in your work right along. Can you talk about that ?

ER: I was very affected by the feminist movement of the 70's and the politics of protest from the 1960's. However, my training as an artist was very traditional.

JB: What do you mean?

ER: I received a Bachelor of Fine Arts in print making at a school where there was one female faculty member. There was little support for my work except from the other students. In school we worked on landscapes, self-portraits, abstractions, still lives. It was a traditional training. At the same time, there was the political activity of the late 60's; people were protesting, organizing, taking drugs and going to parties. Only after leaving school did it occur to me that my experience was unlike that of my teachers. My training as an artist in color, form and space had nothing to do with the subject of my work. At this time, I was very affected by the feminism and the political and social activism of the artwork that was coming out of California.

JB: Anybody in particular you want to mention? You mean, for example, *Womanhouse*?

ER: *Womanhouse.* Some of the early California performance artists like Suzanne Lacey and Barbara Smith. There were many people who were doing work about identity, sexuality, and the place of women in society. I was strongly affected by that work. It gave me permission to go ahead; I began performing. It was something new, it was a new way of speaking.

JB: Did you feel that it was uncharted territory? I remember in some of your early performances I had the sense of you feeling your way along, almost presenting tableaux — very quiet, very slow, very thoughtful examinations of gender. There was a work, and I don't remember the title, where you appeared in a black slip?

ER: *Episodes.*

JB: And I remember sitting there thinking this is a woman who comes out of territory that is only too charted and too overdetermined and she's trying to figure out how to proceed. That's actually close to a title you used for another work.

ER: *She Wants to Understand How to Get from One Place to Another.* In *Episodes.* I wore cardboard high heels strapped to my feet, and I had drawn cardboard arms. There were direct references to prescribed femininity, and my own sense of difficulty of fitting within that prescription. The reason my sexuality was indeterminate in many of the public performance pieces was I wanted to reject a socially accepted definition of femininity and the notion that as a woman you would never dare transgress the confinement of established boundaries. Dressing with an indeterminate sexuality allowed me greater freedom. This is nothing new; historically woman have dressed as men for that exact reason. Somehow in drag I was able to perform on the street, or in the subways. I never would have been able to do these performances in a skirt, heels, and a silk blouse.

JB: You did this in *Man on the Street* and *Subway/Rebus*. It was still uncommon at the time you performed *Man on the Street*. Now, of course in the last couple of years, everything is cross-dressed. But at the time, 1980, there was still a real shock to people who saw you; people who didn't know you would do a double and triple take to try to figure out who you were, and what you were, and how to be comfortable with it.

ER: It's still a shocking act, because it suggests a social critique. It questions the rationale for certain codes of behavior and dress. When you don't subscribe to these codes it raises questions and everyone who's around you is suddenly on an unstable surface, or in an unfamiliar, uncharted landscape...

JB: For the people who are watching, it does have the effect of putting them in a state of not knowing, so that they may be open to suggestion.

ER: I hope that suddenly the questions become larger: why are we standing as a group on the street with many people whom we don't know watching someone pouring detergent on the sidewalk? And then possibly — why don't we do this more often?

JB: Why don't we stand together in groups?

ER: Yes, why don't we stand together in groups? Why don't we talk to each other? What is the nature of public discourse and public social exchange? Why is it so confining? Why are people at such remove from one another? Those kinds of questions are what surround those very public performances.

JB: In your performances your protagonist often seems to go through various border crossings — male/female, public/private, even what you might call normal/deranged — and the spaces in your installation set up borders as well. I'm thinking of the way people huddle in a constructed space to see through the wall in an excerpt from the Anne Frank Project to watch the videotape. Or the bending, stretching and climbing you asked people to do when looking at *Measuring with Eyes and Feet.* I saw those enterprises as being somewhat similar; they achieve the aim that you just described.

ER: It's also a question of how far people are willing to participate as viewers of art. In *Measuring with the Eyes and Feet* (Fig.35), I wanted to subvert the expectation of where art should be located— in the center of the wall under lights. The subject of the work was where women located themselves in urban/architectural space. And so I took down the lighting track. I placed objects at the ceiling, around corners, between a false gallery wall and the window. Text for the installation was adhered with wax to the edge of the molding at six inches above floor level. The type size was small and could be read only by bending over. The objects at the ceiling could be seen in part from below because they were sitting on glass shelves. But you had to climb ladders and stick your head between the beams for a very private kind of viewing experience to see the objects as they were meant to be seen. The work demanded a physical response. There were people who were afraid to climb the ladders. Women were taking off their heels so they were able to climb. There was a sense of challenge. Some people maintained a viewing distance of several feet and missed the work entirely.

JB: The larger questions that you are hoping to suggest to people center on our usual patterns of behavior and social interaction.

ER: Right. I'm hoping that people will start questioning their relationship to art, their assumptions about where they expect to find it, about the distance at which they are supposed to view and not touch.

JB: From an early work, *She Wants to Understand How to Move from One Place to Another*, to the recent *Handwriting Analysis* (Fig.32) in the Anne Frank Project, there's a sustained interest in language. I'm curious what your thoughts are on that.

ER: Language. Well, speaking and reading are two ways in which we learn. I've always been a reader. Growing up, I felt isolated. Books were important companions. Being able to enter another world through words was magic. I didn't have that experience watching television, but I sometimes did with film. My earliest and most sustained means of travel was through words.

Also words are labels. They form categories. They're the means by which we organize and name. Labeling, naming, categorizing have always had a fascination for me. Spoken or printed language is a way of being able to talk about things outside of the language of images, which is the area where artists have been relegated. As an artist you inhabit the world of images. Language is a bridge to other worlds. It's a powerful act to name or to label or to use language as an artist.

JB: So it works in several different ways. In your early work the categorizing function of language was what seemed to be uppermost in your mind. It was a kind of resistance. You were pushing categories like gender away, and resisting oversimple or overdetermined categories.

ER: I'm also very much attracted by the letter and letter forms visually. For example, in the works where I used wooden type, it was the visual representation of language that interested me. Language has a physical presence and a visual presence that's compelling. My father was interested in old signs, shop signs, and he used to give us cast metal letters for birthday presents. He had a collection of circus poster broadsides, 19th century for the most part, some 18th century. Through his interests I was aware of the beauty of letters and the printed form of language. Also, I worked as a graphic designer and type design was central to that work.

JB: You make the language itself a spectacle in a way. There is something to be contemplated in several ways at once. You make language a part of the world of sensation and vision.

ER: Language is the vernacular. It's what exists between people. It's the way that people speak to one another. Incorporating it into my work is another effort at speaking to people.

JB: I have three more questions to ask you and each one of those has to to with ideas raised by people who have written texts for this book. The first question is about an issue raised in Dan Eisenberg's essay and in an essay by Alvin Rosenfeld, "Popularization and Memory: the case of Anne Frank". And that is the issue of how we work towards a sense of the past, and of what role documents and objects can play in writing history. There's a quote from Rosenfeld's article where he says that "he hopes to clarify how on the level of popular perceptions, a sense of the past seems to be shaped less on the basis of information contained in historical documents than through the projection of single elements of ubiquitous and compelling power." Now what he is saying is that these single images lead to vastly over-simplified and tendentious presentations of the past. He's talking in particular about Anne Frank's presentation, both in the United States and Germany, as well as Israel.

ER: And he briefly talked about Japan.

JB: About how each country took her diary, the already edited, presented and published diary and further skewed the information through the translation, through the way the play based on it was then translated and further edited down the text. He also discusses the movie, and how certain presentations of her life were emphasized. In a way this simplifying into single images becomes to him a method of falsifying the past, or denying the past and its complexity. Were these ideas that were important to you in any way as you embarked on the Anne Frank project?

ER: I began with a memory of the text as an adolescent. My experience as a young girl— reading the diary, seeing the play, and the movie— was disturbing. When I returned to the text thirty years later there was a new document to look at, the critical edition of *The Diary of Anne Frank*. This edition, prepared by The Netherlands Institute for War Documentation, contained texts that were part of the original diary but not included in the first publication, information about the Frank family's history and notes on the handwriting analysis. The images of the handwriting analysis were my threshold into the work. This analysis was conducted to substantiate the authenticity of the diary and to determine conclusively Anne Frank's authorship. The idea was to address neo-fascist claims that the diary was a hoax.

In contemporary society there is an overload of information and an insistence on speed. There is no time to dig deeper, to understand the complexity of one's own relationship to this history or these historical events. Because this history is difficult and painful, people need icons or symbols. They want to have an understanding that can be easily contained and shelved. A terrain of unanswerable questions, of unknowable experience, of uncomfortable associations is difficult to negotiate. And people protect themselves from that kind of experience or that level of questioning or knowing. Whole countries and cultures have used Anne Frank as an escape valve. She's become a symbol for people without their having any kind of self exploration or real understanding of her experience.

JB: When you say that as a girl the experience of reading the diary, of seeing the play and the movie was disturbing—what about it was disturbing?

ER: The book was given to me to provide a role model. The first time I read *The Diary* there was no information regarding her experience after the arrest. That was an unarticulated horror. Here was an intelligent, talented young Jewish girl who never got the chance to grow up. In that way she is a confusing role model.

JB: It was given to you as sort of a character model, as how one's character should be?

ER: Yes. *The Diary of Anne Frank* and the story of Harriet Tubman were both books that were given to me as examples of admirable and emulative behavior.

JB: You were put in a bind in the case of Anne Frank, because hers is an arrested development. In a way, it was just character outside history. One was supposed to have these character traits outside any time or any events that happened to you.

ER: Right. It just terrified me because I never felt up to the task. I wasn't going to be able to sneak back in the plantations and lead people to liberation, or be intelligent and courageous while constantly facing arrest and deportation. *The Diary* as originally published portrays Anne in a singular fashion. Other things that I might have related to during adolescence were edited out of the diary.

JB: When you recently found the critical anthology, what moved you to pick that up, to read it? Were you still interested in Anne Frank?

ER: No, it was my husband's family history; they were in Europe during the war. His mother went through the concentration camp system and his father was in Soviet labor camps. It's their experience and Dan's film work which deals with his experience of this particular history that has influenced and affected me. I bought the critical edition for him as a birthday present, took it back and have been working from it ever since. Initially, it was the images of the handwriting analysis that really drew me.

JB: Was the handwriting analysis interesting to you for all the reasons that we've been talking about, such as its graphic complexity?

ER: The graphic quality, the language of science imposed over the language of the hand. This questioning, the necessity to prove someone's existence—and the authenticity. The question of authenticity was very provocative and compelling.

JB: The second question that I have for you is that in her essay Lynne Cooke suggests a parallel between Christa Wolf's writing, her investigation of memory and forgetting with regards to history, and your working process, in particular the way you use original and duplicate materials to invite questions of truth, and duplicity. Lynne Cooke explicitly says that both Wolf and you have a moral code of artistic behavior rather than aesthetics regulated by the senses, and that this moral code informs your art. Do you agree with that?

ER: One likes to think of oneself as a moral person and that one's work and reason for working is tied to a code of ethics and that this informs your activity as an artist. Recently, Christa Wolf's history has unraveled in a very public fashion through the disclosure of her collaboration with the Stasi. This is a case in point. The artist is not exempt. The artist is not pure. It is a romantic notion of the artist to think of her as a heroine. The artist is as susceptible to making the same kinds of mistakes as she may be skilled at critiquing or discussing them. The tragedy of Christa Wolf may be that for so many people she personally was held up as an example. For a German, perhaps someone who grew up in the former East Germany, one needed to believe in Christa Wolf as a symbol. My experience as an American is quite different. But we are all fallible— capable of making mistakes and forgetting our mistakes. I don't see her work as duplicitous. I think that the areas that she describes or explores in her work are significant. And the fact that she was a collaborator and forgot being a collaborator seems true and human.

JB: So in a way it's a lesson to viewers or to readers not to heroicize the artist and not to suspend your own moral code when looking at work.

ER: One shouldn't expect the artist to be the voice of truth. It's just another voice. And that it doesn't relieve the viewer of the responsibility to question. In fact, it underlines it.

JB: At the beginning of her essay, Cindi Katz sets out by saying that she's going to look at your work in terms of geographic scale, and the ways you investigate scale through a number of your works. The reason that she thinks this is important is that by challenging and investigating different constructions of scale that exist already, you release our imagination into new spaces, new ways of moving and existing in time, and that the purpose of that, from her point of view, is social change. Do you share that aim?

ER: Yes. She's looking at the work from her standpoint as a geographer. Pushing against boundaries, performing in public spaces, locating work in places that demand a level of participation from the viewer, speaking directly about woman's experience of architectural and urban space, and trying to describe what that space consists of, how it's defined, resisting the social definition of where women belong, or what their world should consist of— all of that is an effort to redefine, to ask other people to question what is expected or where we belong. There are so many sign posts that let you know whether you belong somewhere, or whether you're an outsider and you don't belong, and who belongs together. That level of confinement has always been something that I want to resist. It's a kind of categorization that's boring. It usually defines like with like, and it's a very superficial reading of social groups. It's more interesting to have diversity.

The potential for change has to do with going against the grain of social expectation. Not all the time, but enough of the time so that you're not located where you're supposed to be. You're required to decide where you want to be and who you want to be with. I never felt that there was a place for me or for my work in the institutions. Whether it was in art school which I was repeatedly advised to leave by people who felt threatened by my work or by my presence, or in museums that had no program or context for it. Necessity demanded that I find other places for the work and for my life as an artist. It would have been an accommodation to give up. And that was the only option that was offered to me, to be relegated to such a marginal existence that there was no room or support to work or to make work. And so if I was going to continue, it necessitated an exploration of other spaces and other audiences. There was such a dynamic, an excitement when I did that. It worked. And then that in itself became a subject of the work.

JB: So once again, it's not that you set up an agenda or a strategy to effect social change so much as you were living through the need yourself, personally, to find new ways of working and new ways of thinking.

ER: Right. It was a question of survival. ■

Figures 6-17 (next four pages):
Those Which Are Most Common
1989
twelve panels, $30^{1}/_{8}$ in. x $22^{1}/_{8}$ in.
handmade paper
with linoleum block prints

Installation at the
DeCordova Museum,
Lincoln, Massachusetts

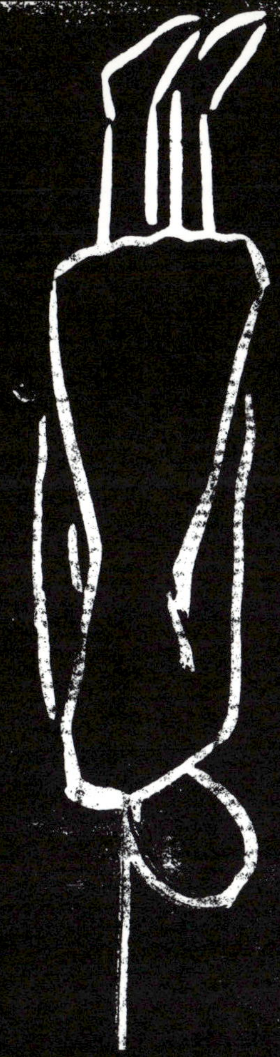

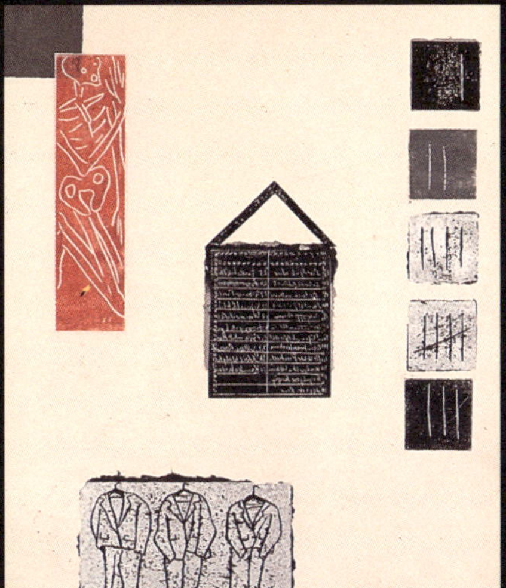

Fig.6

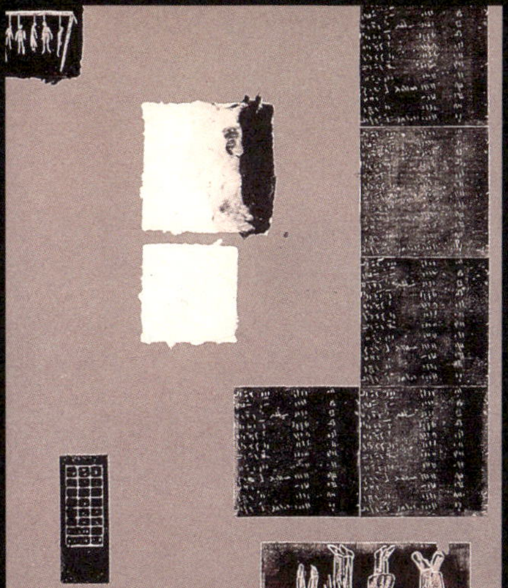

Fig.7

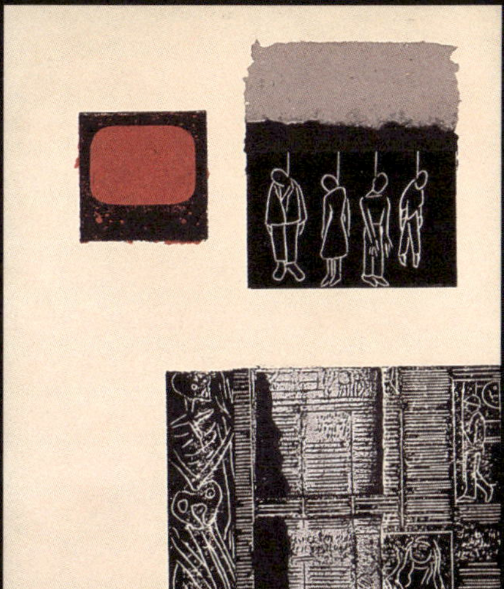

Fig.8

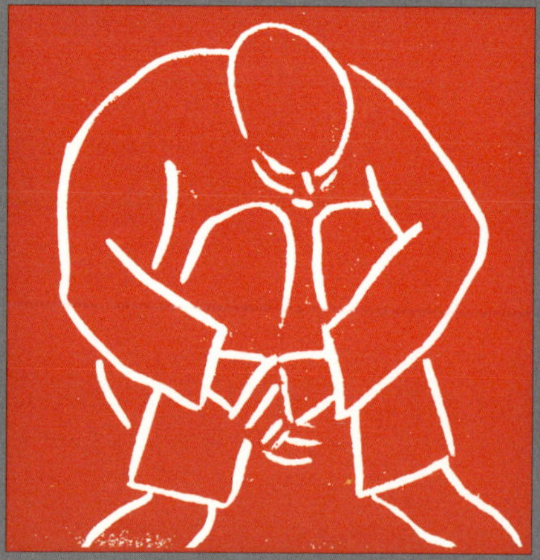

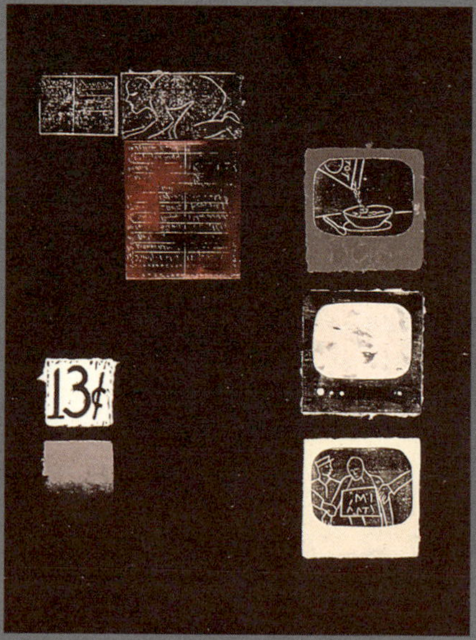

Fig.9

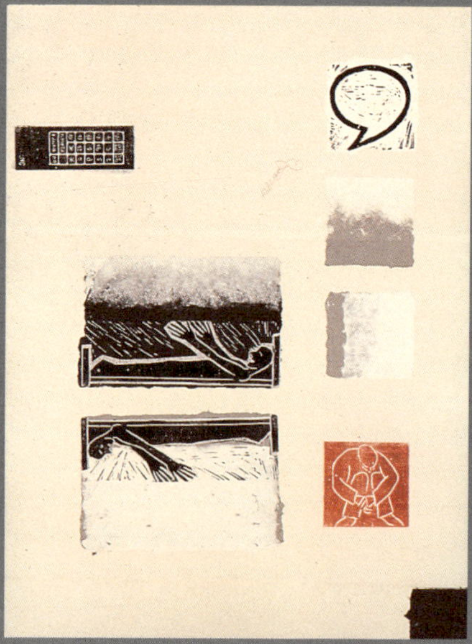

Fig.10

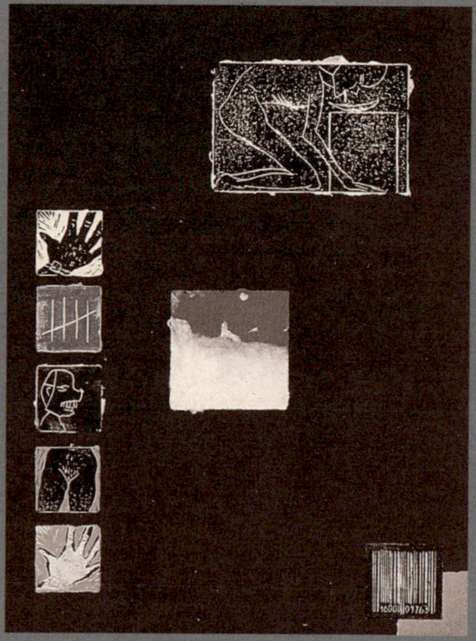

Fig.11

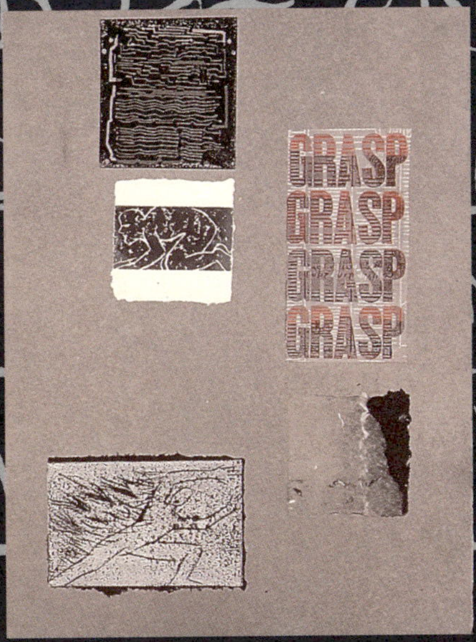

Fig.12

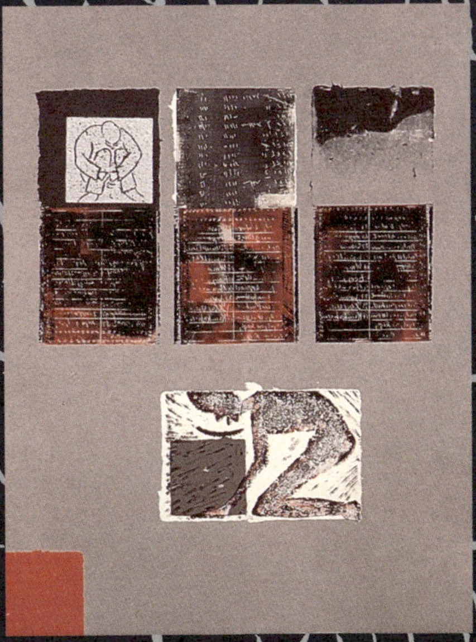

Fig.13

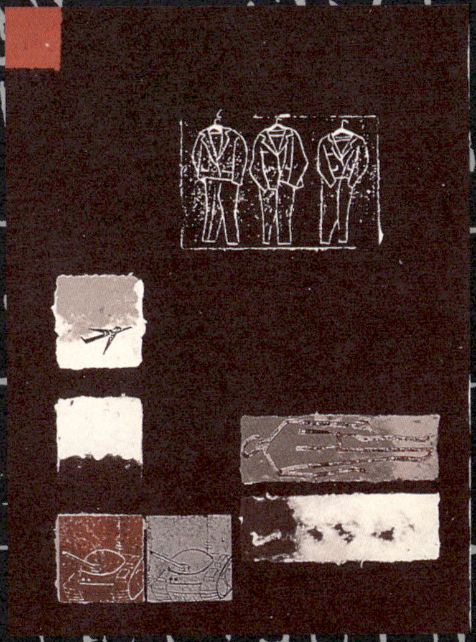

Fig.14

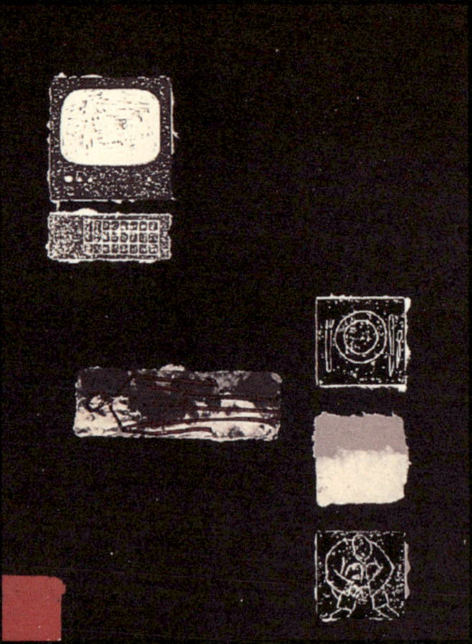

Fig.15

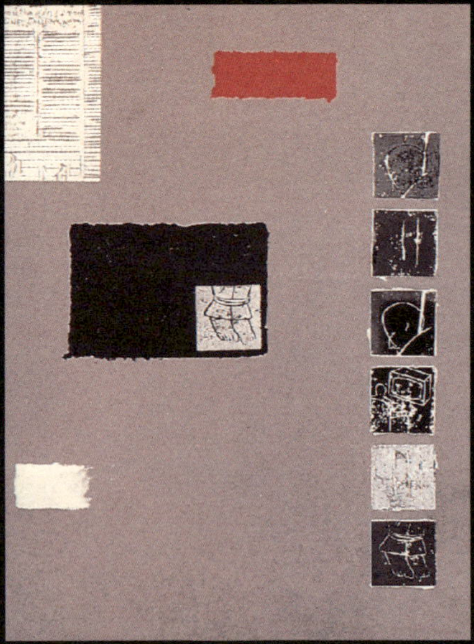

Fig.16

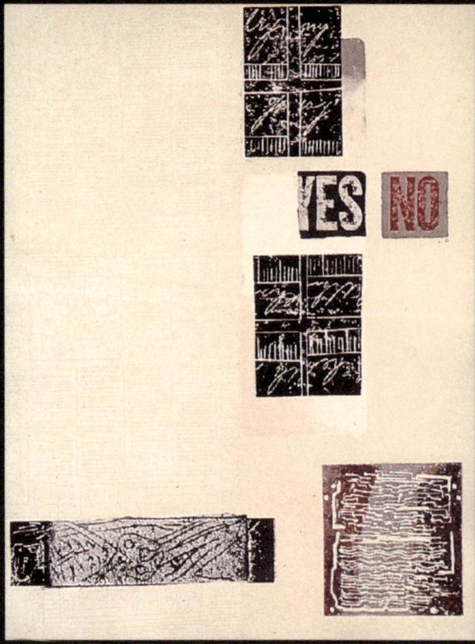

Fig.17

DEPARTMENT OF CORRECTION: NOTES ON ELLEN ROTHENBERG'S *THOSE WHICH ARE MOST COMMON*

BY DAN EISENBERG

In 1988, after completing a series of drawings formally derived from Mexican picture novellas and Chinese opera books, Ellen Rothenberg worked with the paper-makers at Rugg Road Papers to produce a series of handmade sheets that would be used for "future" projects. One set of these papers, a series of twelve large base sheets with various overlays of smaller colored paper frames in gray, black, white, and red would become *Those Which Are Most Common*. Although the sheets were produced independently of the images that would later appear on them and devised strictly according to formal considerations, the *tabula rasa* of the sheets began a process of collecting images and ideas that would occupy Rothenberg for the next few years. In this context *Those Which Are Most Common* can be seen as a notational device for the working out of images, ideas, gestures, and details that would find further revision and development in *Partial Index*, *A Probability Bordering On Certainty*, and other works of the early 1990's.

What was set into motion in *Those Which Are Most Common* is the specific matrix of history and documentation, their mediation through form, and the placing of the individual in the current of historical events. As a large and irresoluble set of questions on the nature of historical experience, the artworks generated from this matrix remain provisional responses, meditations on the range of possible relationships.

The individual images that comprise *Those Which Are Most Common* are a series of linoleum block prints that are used in thematic and formal variation within the twelve panels. The images run the range from the leaves of a calendar, a computer bar-code, the remote control from a TV set and other visual details of everyday life, to television images from the evening news, particularly those relating to the student uprising at Tienamien Square and the hanging body of Lt. Col. William Higgins, direct references to documents such as a list of names from Dachau, and appearing for the first time in Rothenberg's work, a sample from the Netherlands State forensic analysis of Anne Frank's handwriting. These images are put through the formal wringer—

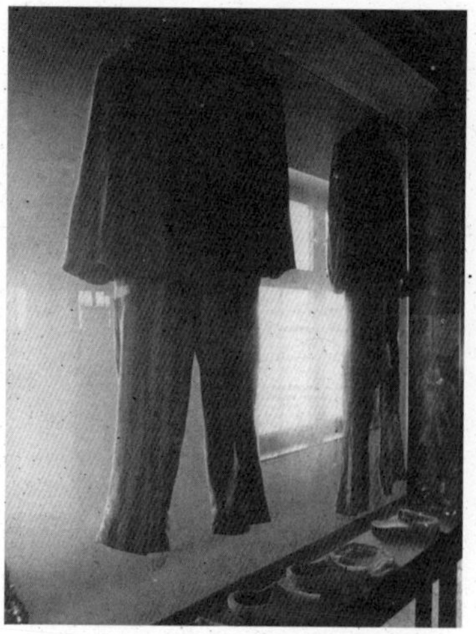

backwards, forwards, upside down, right-side up, positive, negative — a virtual compendium of variations that cannot be read in any prescribed order.

Formally, *Those Which Are Most Common* shares much with Rothenberg's performance and "time-based" works. The twelve panels do not function as independent entities, but as fragments of a whole. Although compositional solutions exist within each panel, the true form of the work is only revealed when all panels are seen together. This development depends on time, on the relation of images in one panel to those in another. The narrative progression, although somewhat more open, is similar to that in Rothenberg's video and performance works where images operate according to iconic associations and where meaning derives from a peculiar sensibility of accretion and accumulation. An innocuous image such as the computer bar-code suddenly becomes sinister when an image of lists from Dachau is close at hand. Proximity and context both determine and transform meaning, specifying a range of associations.

The work is experientially porous, indeterminate. There's lots of space between images; between panels one must take a leap, engage in a constant revision of meanings. A revision that requires one not only to "revise" but also "to see again."

The hanging suit and the hanging men provide an interesting model for how meaning occurs in the work. Rothenberg has said that the hanging suit is a quote from Joseph Beuys's *Felt Suit* (Fig.19) of 1970 . But many images of hanging exist within the piece, each with multiple possible sources. Beuys' own image could very well have derived from the suits hanging at the Dachau Memorial Museum (Fig.18), reproduced in the museum catalog. In place of the hanging man the suit embodies the absent man. Other images of suits on hangers may very well have come from Rothenberg's own studio, with her costumes on racks suspended in the air, embodiments of her own alternate identities. She has long been fascinated by the transformative qualities of

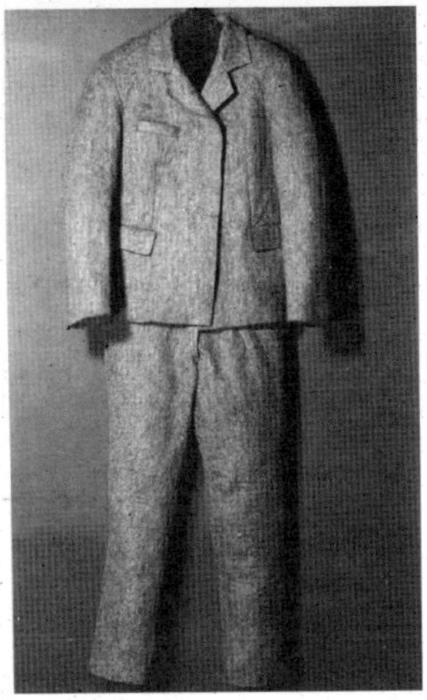

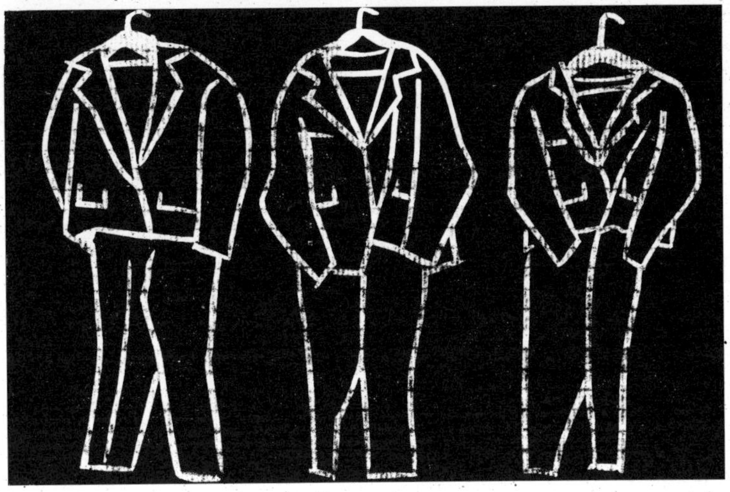

Figure 18 (left):
prisoner uniform,
Dachau Museum
reproduced in
Concentration Camp Dachau 1933-1945
Brussels, 1978

Figure 19 (center):
Joseph Beuys, *Felt Suit*, 1970
Courtesy of
Busch-Reisinger Museum
Harvard University
Art Museums, Cambridge, Massachusetts
Purchase in memory of
Eda K. Loeb

Figure 20 (right):
Detail from panel nine
of *Those Which Are Most Common*, 1989

clothing, shoes, gloves. Their multiple appearances in the range of her work evokes the body in both corporeal and psychological presence. Add to this the image of the hanging feet of Lt. Col. William Higgins, an American soldier working in Lebanon under the auspices of the U.N. who was kidnapped and hung by Islamic Fundamentalists in 1989, and a necessary iconographic density is achieved.

If I may use a rhetorical description of the general method, there is a metonymic compression in the selection of images — the choices are spare, yet each image retains a visual language potential that is wide and variable. There is then a parataxic construction within and between panels; panels are composed to a logic that is beyond normal narrative conventions, and one is confronted with relations and juxtapositions that are at once ordered and random — one is unsure at times which.

This kind of open construction demands a highly active engagement on the part of the viewer. It is here, in the world of reception, that a kind of "hermeneutic" activity occurs. And this interpretive engagement is essential, for the images have multiple glosses and sources. It's in the cross-points of memory and association that the piece is energized.

There is a fascination here with both the document and its transmission device, whether it be a newspaper, a TV, or an archival document. The choice of

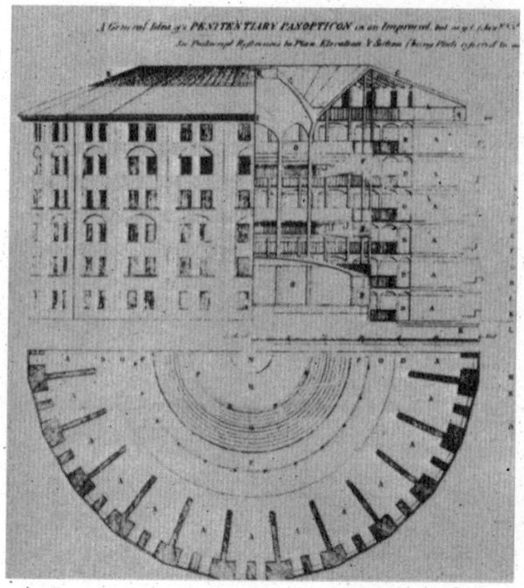

linoleum block images alludes to earlier political usage of the graphic image, in particular political broadsides and the twentieth century expressionist woodcuts of Kollwitz, Barlach, Munch, Kirschner, Nolde, Heckel, and Schmidt-Rotluff.

The earliest forms of paper and printing technology are used to great ironic effect; an interesting dissonance occurs when one views these contemporary images rendered in antique form. The suggestion is of a long, dark historical record predicated on disaster and death that extends into our computer age. But there is also a stillness and silence that reminds one of the great Eastern block printing tradition, providing a grander scale of historical time as well. All of these seemingly contradictory articulations raise important fundamental questions. What is a document? How does memory work? What is historical, how do we differentiate between personal and public spheres? Where are the divisions?

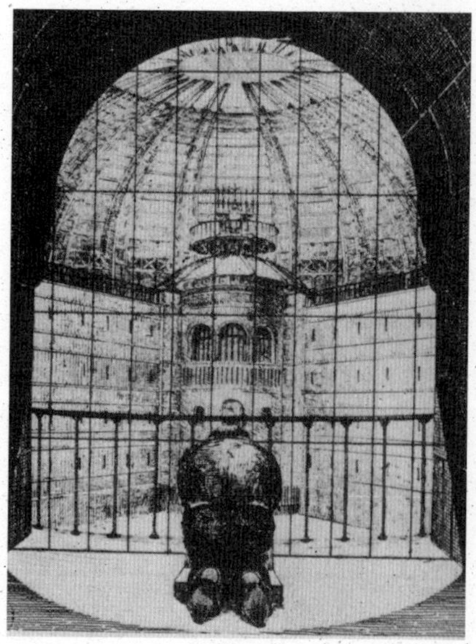

By using "frames" within the panels as a formal device, *Those Which Are Most Common* recalls both the pictographic narrative methods of comic books and the storyboards of cinema. But it is the image of the prisoner caught within the confines of his "frame" that reveals perhaps the most essential nexus of the piece.

Michel Foucault has keenly pointed out in *Discipline and Punish* that a significant transition in the history of incarceration was the advent of the Panoptic Prison of Jeremy Bentham in the late 18th century (Fig.21). In this architectural model, a central core stands as an observational tower within an annular building, with a multi-tiered ringing of cells around the imposing central structure. The cells have two windows, one large opening facing the tower, the other on the opposite end of the cells allowing light to pass through. "By the effect of backlighting, one can observe from the tower, standing out precisely against the light, the small captive shadows in the cells of the periphery. They are like so many cages, so many small theaters, in which each

Figure 21: Jeremy Bentham
plan of the Panopticon
The Works of Jeremy Bentham,
ed. Bowring vol. IV, 1843. 172-3

actor is alone, perfectly individualized." One of the salient characteristics of the observational tower is that through a system of visual baffles, the observer is invisible to the observed. The prisoner never knows who is watching or when surveillance takes place, with a concomitant psychological pressure to "self-correct". In this space authority is localized yet anonymous, power derives through omniscience and the potential for response and thus becomes the architectural model for the state itself.

What is so interesting about the Panoptic Prison is that it is designed with full awareness of the fact that Barker was constructing at exactly the same period (the first seems to be around 1787) "Panoramas in which visitors, occupying a central place, saw unfolding around them a landscape, a city, or a battle." The visitors occupied exactly the place of the sovereign gaze of Bentham's Panopticon.

Figure 22: N. Harou-Romain
plan for a penitentiary, 1840
a prisoner in his cell kneeling at
prayer before the central
inspection tower.

Many of these panoramic spaces still exist. In Boston, the Battle of Gettysburg was presented in a panoramic space now housing the Boston Center for the Arts. This travelling historical spectacle appeared throughout the US in huge cylindrical buildings with domed ceilings specially built for viewing panoramic tableaux with accompanying spectacles of sound and light.

The oscillation from surveillance to observation to spectacle through the means of architecture suggests a deeper connection than one would be inclined to embrace. The power of the observer, the power of observation itself, is an enlightenment evolution from the application of regal or monarchic power. It obtains from a whole history of new discovery linked to the senses, a science based on sensual differences. That knowledge is power is implicit in this new system, but the abuse of power has its source in knowledge as well, through the control of information and its manipulation.

In its presentation at the DeCordova Museum in 1989 (Fig.23), *Those Which Are Most Common* was exhibited within the curved walls of a "watch-tower"

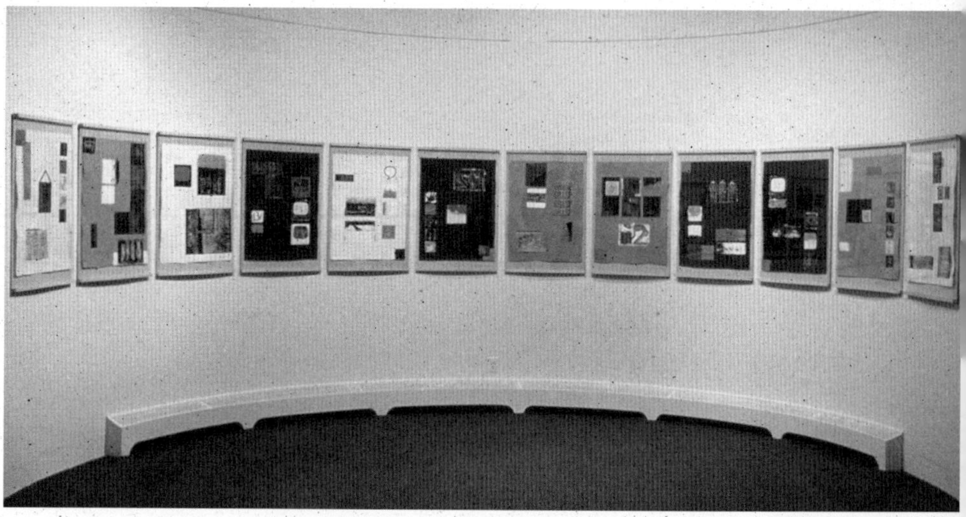

Figure 23:
Those Which Are Most Common, 1989
view of the installation at the DeCordova Museum, Lincoln, Massachusetts

structure, part of the architectural detailing of the museum, recapitulating both Bentham's Panoptic Prison and Barker's panoramic spaces of the 19th century. Here the shuttling between surveyor, observer, and authority creates a complicated domain of knowledge, experience, responsibility. It can be disconcerting to place oneself in the central viewing position of this work, for the architecture effects feelings of too much responsibility, or of being too much a judge, or too much a witness.

Counting, accounts, lists, tallies are ubiquitous from panel to panel. The roman numerals and fruit-stand numbers have appeared in Rothenberg's work before, as costume elements for her performance characters The Scientist and The Fat Man. Here, the image of *13¢* (Fig.9) which appears in one of the panels is significant beyond its generic quality. It is the value of the single bullet used in the execution of Chinese political prisoners, the amount of the official bill sent to the families of the executed for payment to the state.

The leaves of a calendar tick off the daily balance sheet — this day despair, the next a sense of loss, the following a consideration of one's own value and self-worth. Every accounting is a measure against death, every accounting is measured against death.

With the quotations from the handwriting samples of Anne Frank and the Dachau lists we are reminded of the bureaucratic efficiency of the death industry of the Third Reich, of the reduction of humans into names, numbers, constituent body parts, possessions, and labor. The features of the modern state made and make technocratic control of private daily life a constant threat, and information in all its forms is its most powerful instrument. In *Those Which Are Most Common* Rothenberg not only cautions us to these examples, but by citing contemporary images raises doubts about what can be genuinely known in a world of controlled images.

Will others in the future peruse only those documents of our time retained in archives because they were not willfully destroyed, chosen as the "correct" representations of events or facts; will they view only the documentary icons we were too weak to challenge — the toppling statues, the fleeing refugees, the rolling of tanks, the hanging bodies? We too have seen them all before.

It seems that there is an inherent paradox: images are produced for consumption that have been in some measure pre-read, the conditions for their reception put in place well before their appearance. How then can any new event provide a new image or truly unique information, when what we seek is what we already know? We have only these images in our collective repertoire to instruct both composition and content. The question arises, do the images we see and learn instruct or contain our vision of the world, or do they constantly reassert themselves because we see deeper patterns repeating from generation to generation, from event to event, ad infinitum?

In addition to these ideas is the very real problem of the superfluity of images. How often one feels frozen into an over-stimulated paralysis by the sheer abundance of disturbing images calling for our limited attention, resources, and political will. The double meaning of the empty word-balloon; that of the victim, that of the viewer, addresses this directly. Here we are, fluctuating between confusion, resolve, commitment and despair.

Is this a cul-de-sac of irresoluble conflicts, a question which has no better answer than what we are presented in everyday life? The work is not so nihilistic as to suggest that the individual doesn't matter. Doesn't it address the individual with a confrontation, of placing oneself within the historical stream? We've long accommodated ourselves to open forms, to a permanent irresolution — with this comes the false suggestion that art's inability to take a stand confirms our own lack of certainty, or commitment, a sign of the more generalized confusion of our time. Instead formal openness helps to define our own judgements, not as a mirror but as a series of self-interrogations — each fragment requires a processing of information, of an appropriate context, of an active consciousness. The search for solutions is implicit in the construction principles at work in the piece. Redemption is in the knowledge that we still are connected by a moral thread — our real mutual history.

It is in this spirit that the open-formed artwork sees alienation as an open door to discipline, responsibility, and action. ■

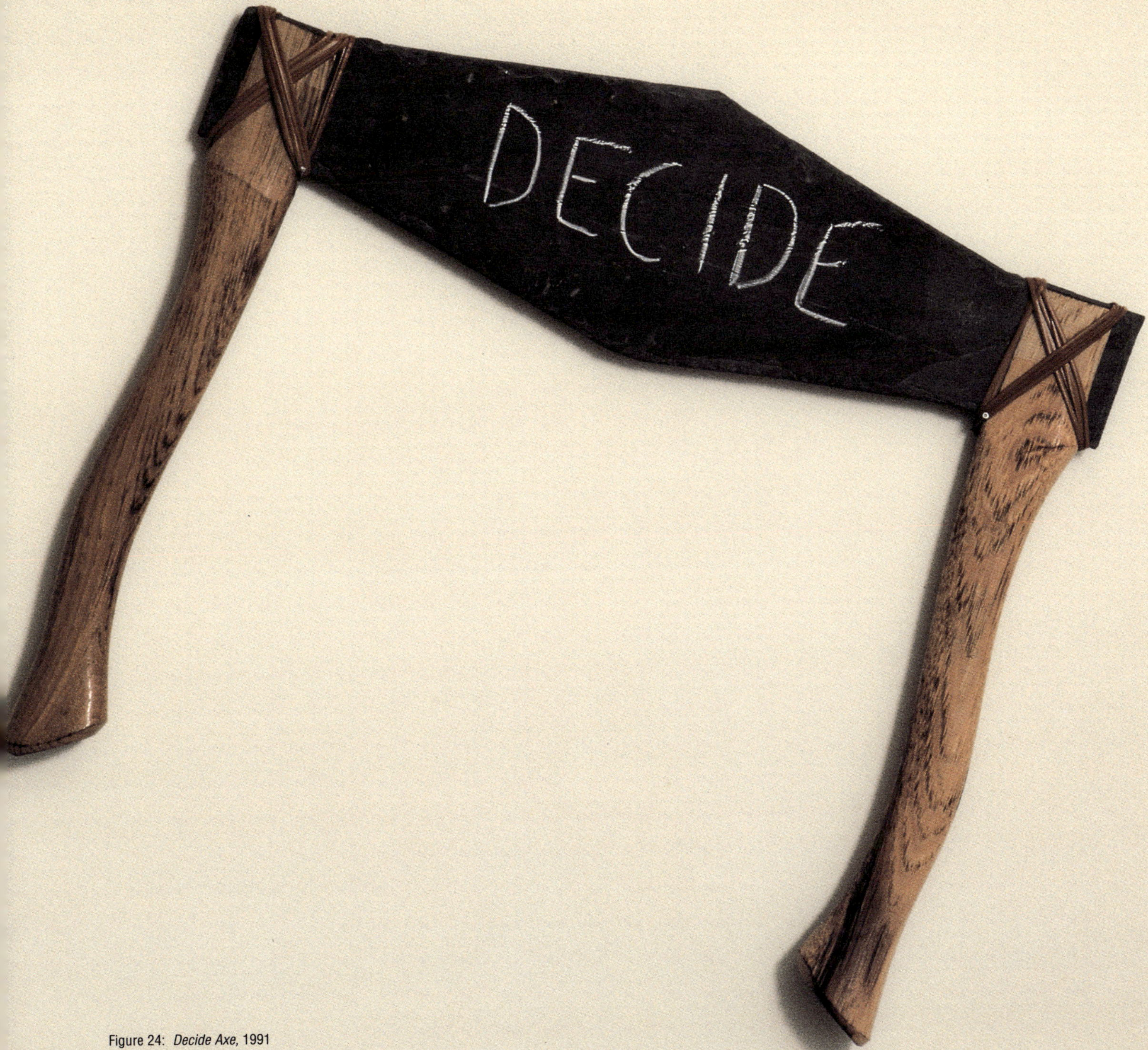

Figure 24: *Decide Axe,* 1991
object from installation
Measuring With the Eyes and Feet
14 in. x 17 in. x 1 1/4 in.
wood, slate and leather

Installation at the
Howard Yezerski Gallery,
Boston, Massachusetts

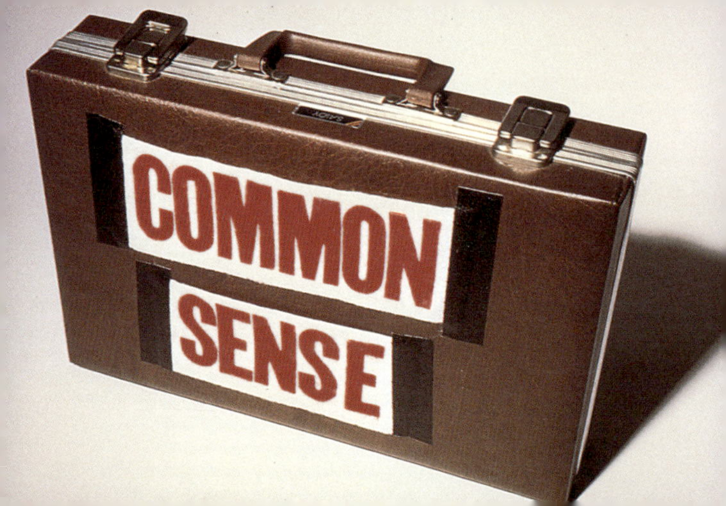
COMMON
SENSE

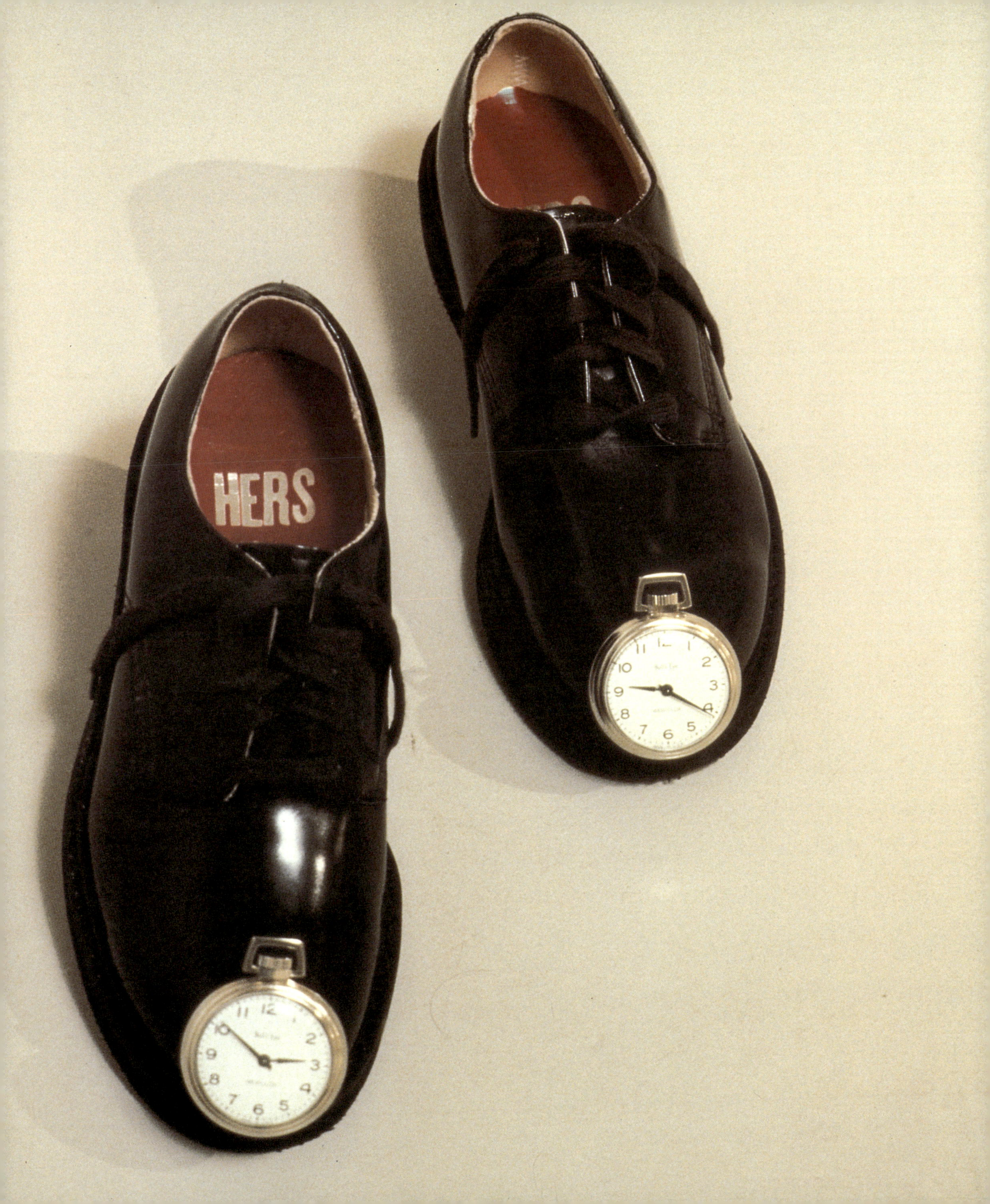
HERS

Figure 27:
The German Question, 1992
performance prop from *Hello Traitor*
4 in. x 4 1/2 in. x 3/4 in.
plastic and printed cardboard

Performance at Festival Giannozzo,
Berlin, Germany

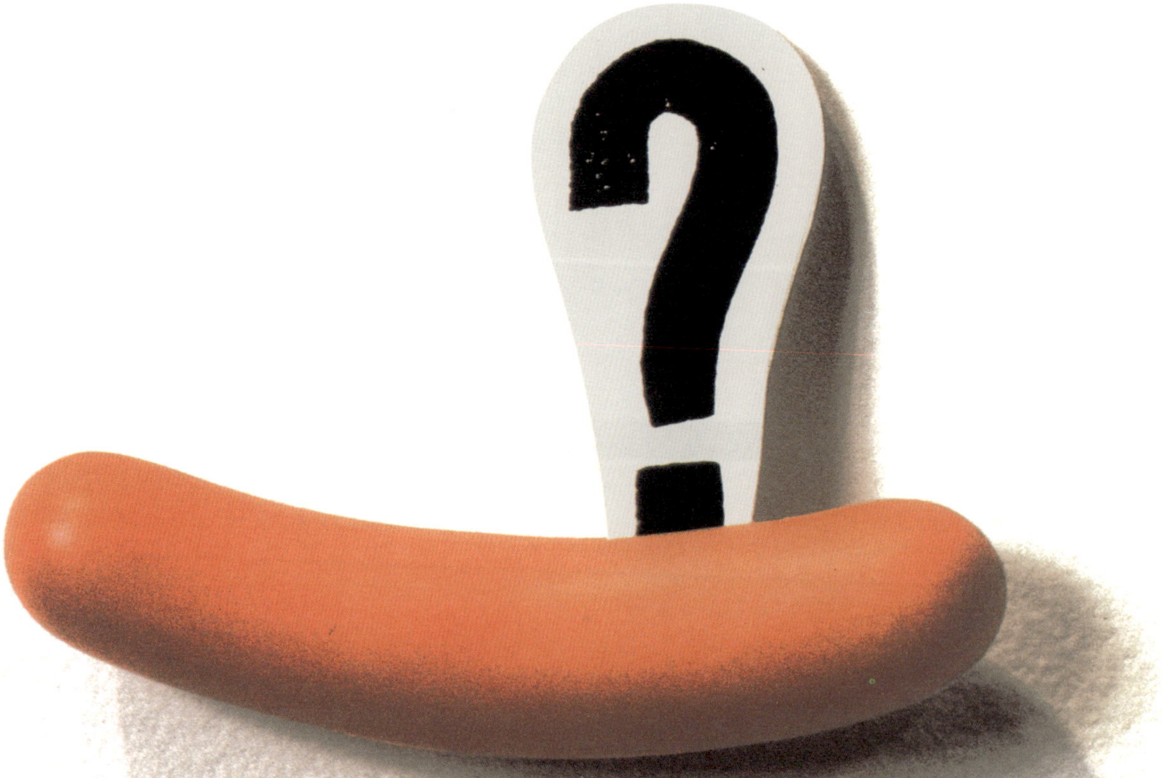

"She wants to understand how to move from one place to another"

Spaces of Possibility/ Spaces of Change: the personal geography of Ellen Rothenberg

by Cindi Katz

Geographic scale is a means of staging the world and situating oneself in it. Scale is often understood descriptively as a hierarchical scheme for ordering space, but the production of scale is an inherently political act wherein the multiple arenas of social life are constituted and identity is negotiated. Geographic scale resonates with tension between what is held within a space and the lines drawn between spaces. The socially constructed nature of accepted demarcations such as those between home, body, and community is usually masked by its taken-for-grantedness. A spatially informed politics not only would expose the constructions and seek their origins, but would work in ways that transgress them and produce new spaces that empower more than rein in. This kind of politics is at the core of Ellen Rothenberg's work which produces space both metaphoric and material to call into question and violate the constructed separations between public and private, body and world, lost and found.

Rothenberg's performances and props intrigue and compel me as much for the specific and wonderful ways they produce space as for the way they interrogate and reframe issues at the heart of my work as a cultural geographer and feminist social theorist—orientation, mobility, and control over personal and public space. As

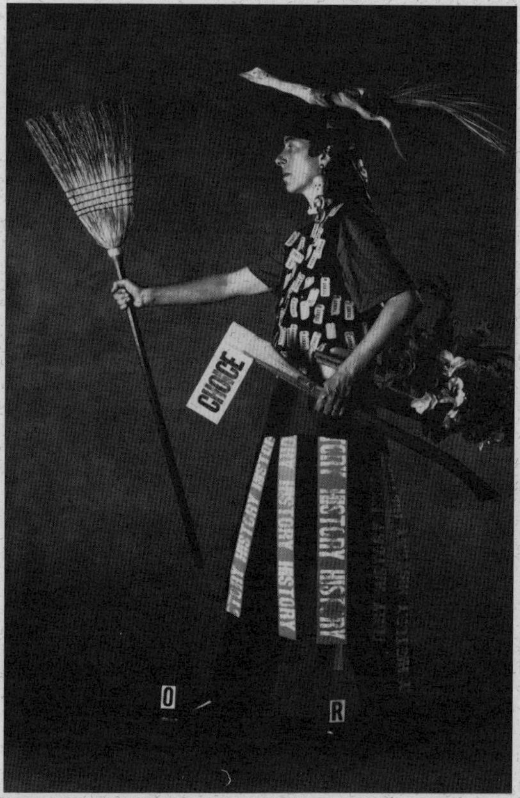

Figure 28: *History or Choice*, 1989
photo collaboration with
Bruce T. Martin
produced in conjunction with the
installation *For the Instruction of Young Ladies*

Installation at the
Rose Art Museum, Brandeis University
Waltham, Massachusetts

Rothenberg charts a course for exploring the meanings and multiple determinations of the identities offered by gender, work, class, and nationality, she undermines any possibility of holding these social locations separate. One of her most telling metaphors, a pair of compass shoes (Fig.34), in the *Landscape Vitrine* from *The Marginal Way* (1990), suggests a means to navigate that continually undermines itself. Perched on stacks of plates and surrounded by the location numbers off telephone poles, the shoes in the vitrine un/settle—wearing them Rothenberg might move but is always already home; her ability to wayfind pivots on her own axis. Likewise in *Speak Speak Speak!* (1987), her ruler shoes (Fig.29) make her body the standard measure. In that piece she literally traces a path that moves but cannot leave home, that travels but finds no safe harbor. Wearing an enormous kimono of stiff paper with "HOME" stencilled all over it, an Asian mask, and a broom as a hat, she trudges along a path, dragging a model of a house, her head framed in a video monitor, grasping a banner stamped "family" in her outstretched hand. To write these words it sounds obvious, but the thrill of Ellen Rothenberg's work is its astonishing subtlety and wry contradictions—the striking beauty of the *Home Kimono* seduces as the "house and chain" jars.

Figure 29: *Ruler Shoes*, 1986
Leather shoes with painted rulers

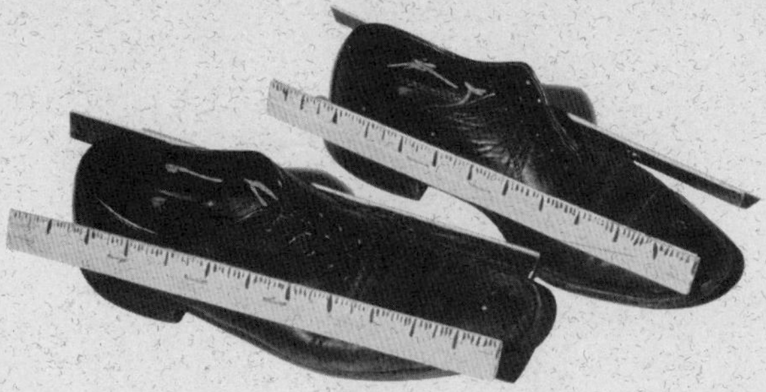

In Rothenberg's work, the pain of everyday life choices is encoded as spatial practice. She stages a kind of representational space so textured and rooted that it allows us, in the words of Henri Lefebvre,[1] "to rediscover time...in and through space." For Lefebvre, this rediscovery, which explicitly recovers the production of space, counters the mystifying fragmentation of modern society. What Lefebvre was after, and Rothenberg provides, was a way of understanding the social in the spatial and the spatial as social relations. He was working against the dominant tendency to compartmentalize—to understand space as a container for discrete objects or as something discontinuous. His project countered conventional knowledge of space that "wavers between description and dissection," because it was "integrated unintentionally into existing society and forced to operate within that society's framework." In *Speak Speak Speak!*, which plays with the simultaneity of fixity and motion, self and otherness, representations and received identities, Rothenberg uses spatial strategies—the tethering of her body to home, the constant framing of her motion—to question that very framework.

Similarly, in (Fig.35) *Measuring with Eyes and Feet* (1991) Rothenberg sets up a series of spatial metaphors to describe the resonances between women's sociospatial marginalization and multiple roles, the ways women are nowhered while having to be everywhere. Ladders lead to glass ceilings on which rest a "motherhood belt," "know/how gloves," and "passion meter underwear." At the foot of the ladders are a purse filled with burned candles and the *Hers Shoes* (Fig.26), a pair of shoes with clocks on the toes, each set to a different time. Time geographers who spent years studying and charting the paths and encounters of people's daily lives and foundered on finding a means to illustrate meaningfully the multiple and competing time-space demands on social actors might draw inspiration from the elegance of the *Hers Shoes* for conveying their insights.

1. Lefebvre, H. *The Production of Space.* Oxford: Basil Blackwell, 1991. p. 91.

Throughout Rothenberg's work, shoes and other props tell stories of encumbered mobility and blurred boundaries. In her public performance, *Man on the Street* (1981), she becomes a deranged man ranting through mundane choices to resolve deeply unsettling problems. Ungrounded, she scrapes in place, grasping at possible futures that perish as they are uttered. The metronome of her cleats at once marks time and scratches at the world. In another part of *The Great Circle* (Fig.1) she wears a papier mâché suit of tabloid front pages. She rolls the "time/money furrower," designed after an early American farming tool — on one side a quarter on the other a clock — shouting "the great circle." Always moving, her newspaper suit encompassing a world and encumbering a body, she goes nowhere, producing a space that traces time as money. In *Vices and Virtues* (1989) bread shoes sit neatly on a series of doormats under aprons inscribed with each of the vices and virtues (Fig.33). Their homey presence transfigures movement to rootedness and binds the domestic to a catalogue of sin and morality.

This move is reversed in her public performance *Hello Traitor* (1992) where the bread shoes insinuate home-made evil. Rothenberg walks through Berlin in the shoes, wearing a man's suit jacket with price tags over the front and a *"verkauft"* (sold) sign on the back. In blond braids dangling from a hat (Fig.30), she frames *The German Question* (Fig.27) — saluting as she raises a plastic hot dog to her mouth. Later in the piece she sweeps a cavernous open space, pushing a giant street broom with the word "voice" mounted on it. In gardening shoes marked "forwards" and "backwards," (Fig.31) she scrapes along in front of a monolithic housing project in the eastern part of Berlin. Her act, which recalls the *Man on the Street* carefully sweeping a patch of sidewalk in a maniacal bid for meaningful presence, makes literal the metaphor of 'municipal housekeeping' through which women, marginalized from production in the nineteenth century, reinserted themselves into public life. This replacement has added urgency in post-war Berlin as Rothenberg marks her presence, her silenced but insistent voice as woman and Jew, in the city.

Figure 30:
German American Hunting Cap
1992
prop from *Hello Traitor*
plaid woolen cap and flax braids.

Figure 31:
Ruckwarts/Vorwarts Shoes
1992
prop from *Hello Traitor*
German gardening clogs and
engraved aluminum labels

Props from performance at
Festival Giannozzo, Berlin, Germany

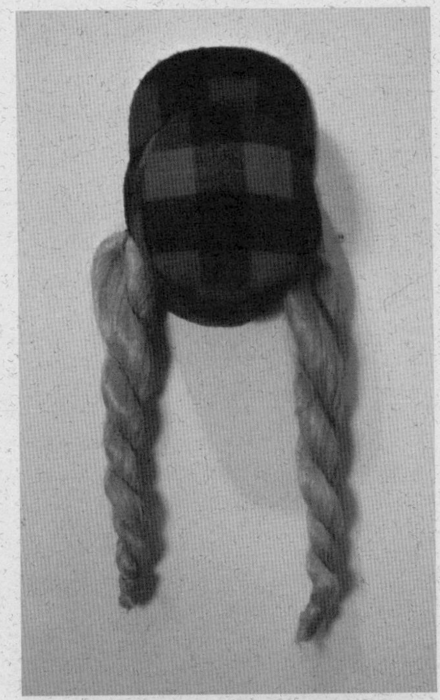

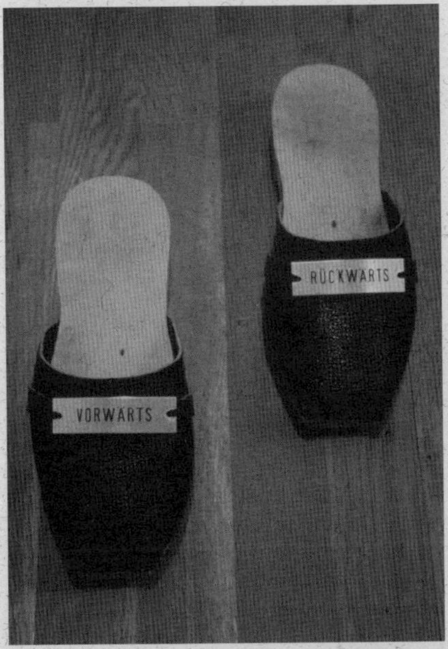

The "backwards and forwards" shoes suggest history as well as geography, and Rothenberg's more recent work moves through time as well as space. Again the course she charts is rooted, embodied, personal and deeply political — not an anonymous history, nor a single trajectory but constantly reworked, multiply traveled paths in which fragments of identity are recovered, foreclosed possibilities reopened. In this project, the diaries of Anne Frank provide a perfect lens to refract the world and position herself in time and space.

In *Partial Index* (1991) Rothenberg's fascination with the written word (Fig.43), the act of writing as an historical and spatial practice, and the marking of space and time as a means to recover memory and the loss of bearing is brought to bear with profound elegance on the case of Anne Frank.

The work is a meditation on indexing as at once a marker of loss and a means of location and retrieval. It turns on the power of the absent presence, simultaneously recovering, documenting, and mapping all the detail of Frank's life as if it could somehow conjure her presence, and building a structure that marks her loss in the traces. This move, of course, subversively reworks the cold efficiency of Nazism— the very tale it tells marks the failure of all their cataloguing and indexing to erase those numbered for extermination, while the piece (and the diary) testify to the singular horrors of their success. Rothenberg attempts to locate herself/Anne—victim/witnesses, subject/objects—in the diary and in contents of the attic quarters that comprised the world of its utterance. The blown up samples of Frank's writing from a handwriting analysis (Fig.32), with arrows showing the direction of her pen stroke, are maps to the irrecoverable site of enunciation. If we pore over them long enough it seems we might at last locate Frank, whose loss is what makes the minutiae of her presence so powerful and important.

It is on the minutiae, the mundane practices and fragments, of everyday life that Ellen Rothenberg's work turns. She is an explorer of her homeland, producing a space that pivots on the inseparable axes of identity, history, and geography. Her explorations are of the ordinary, the elemental—her body in its home space. But the point is that there is no space outside. Rothenberg's insistent scratching, probing, and subverting constantly interrupt the production of her home space as a terrain of terrible limits to glimpse and even create possibilities for undermining the meanings and comforts offered by received identities of gender, class, nation. Her work produces an imaginary, and it constructs a space from which social change is possible. ■

Figure 32:
Handwriting Analysis, 1993
from the installation
A Probability Bordering on Certainty
xerography on silk tissue,
steel brackets.

Installation at
The Mary Ingraham Bunting Institute,
Radcliffe College,
Cambridge, Massachusetts

Collection of Charlene Engelhard

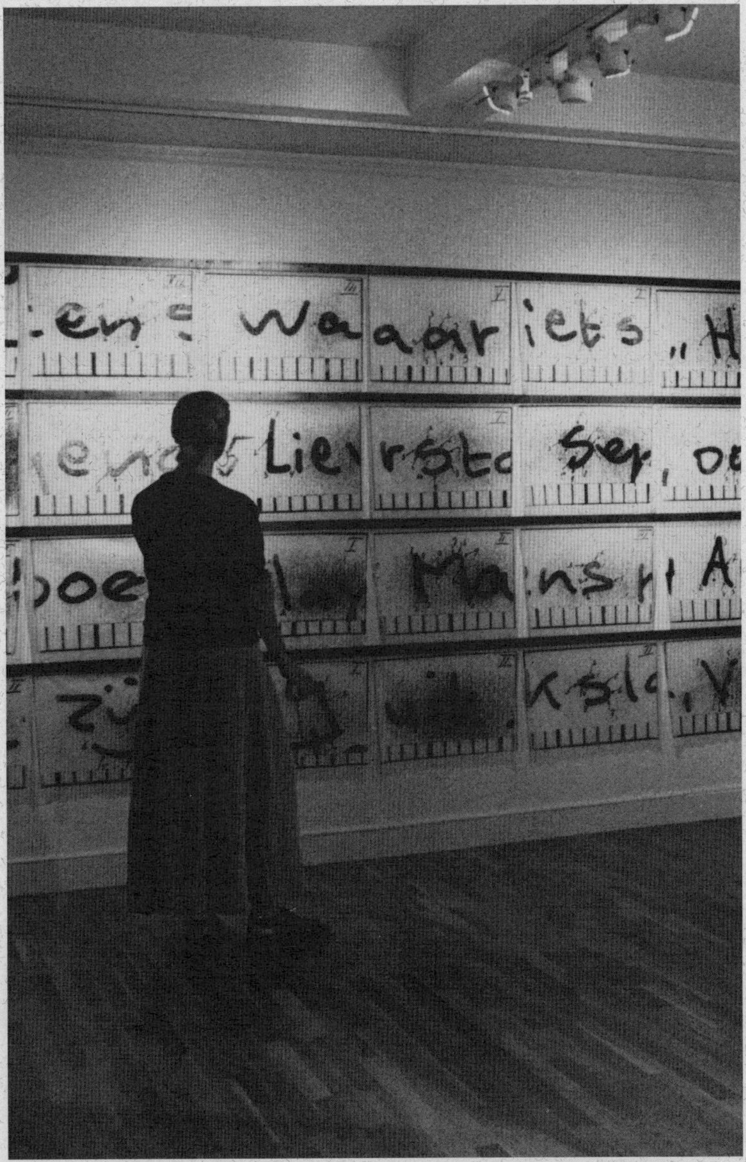

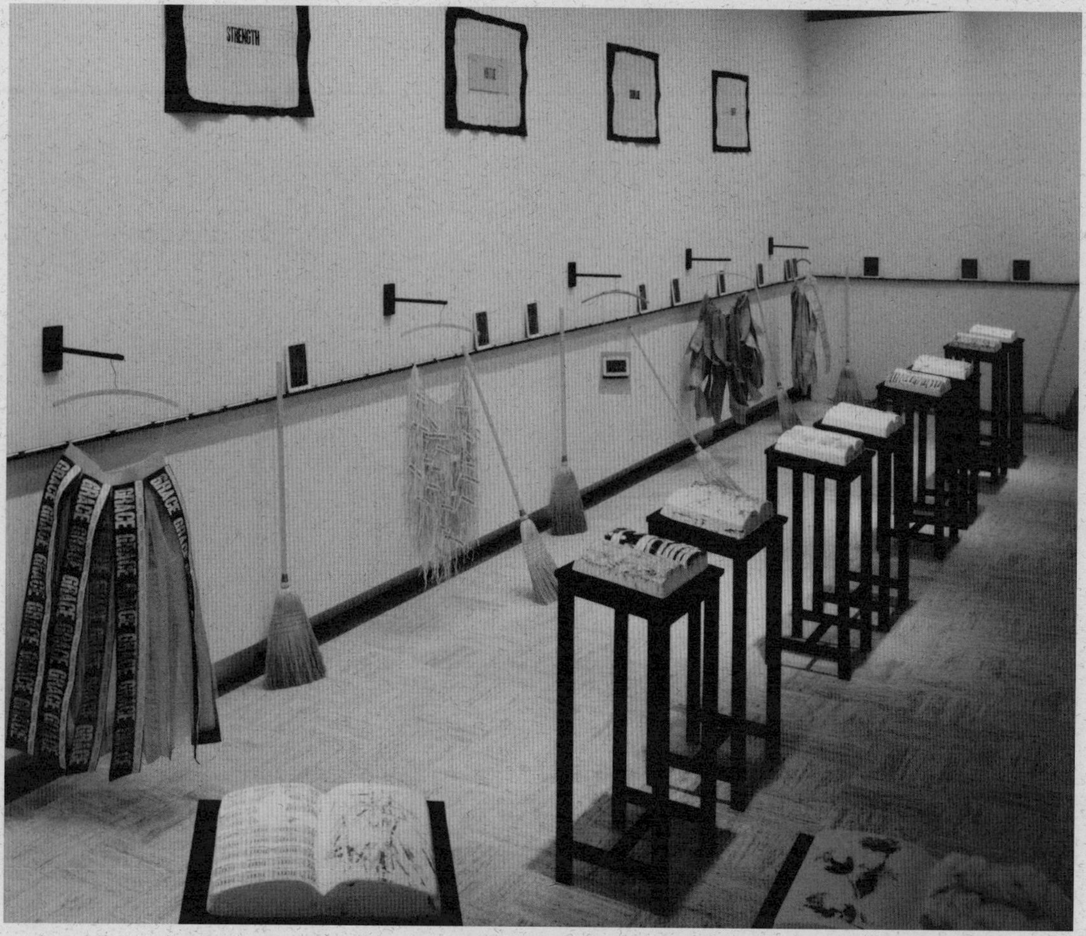

Figure 33: (right)
Vices and Virtues, 1989
from the installation *Speak!*
printed cardboard aprons, bread
shoes, and sisal mats

Installation at
Massachusetts College of Art,
Boston, Massachusetts

(left)
For the Instruction of Young Ladies, 1989
brooms, skirts, blackboard
drawings, "lies" and "beliefs"
pencils, cast books, and
samplers

Installation at Rose Art Museum
Brandeis University,
Waltham, Massachusetts

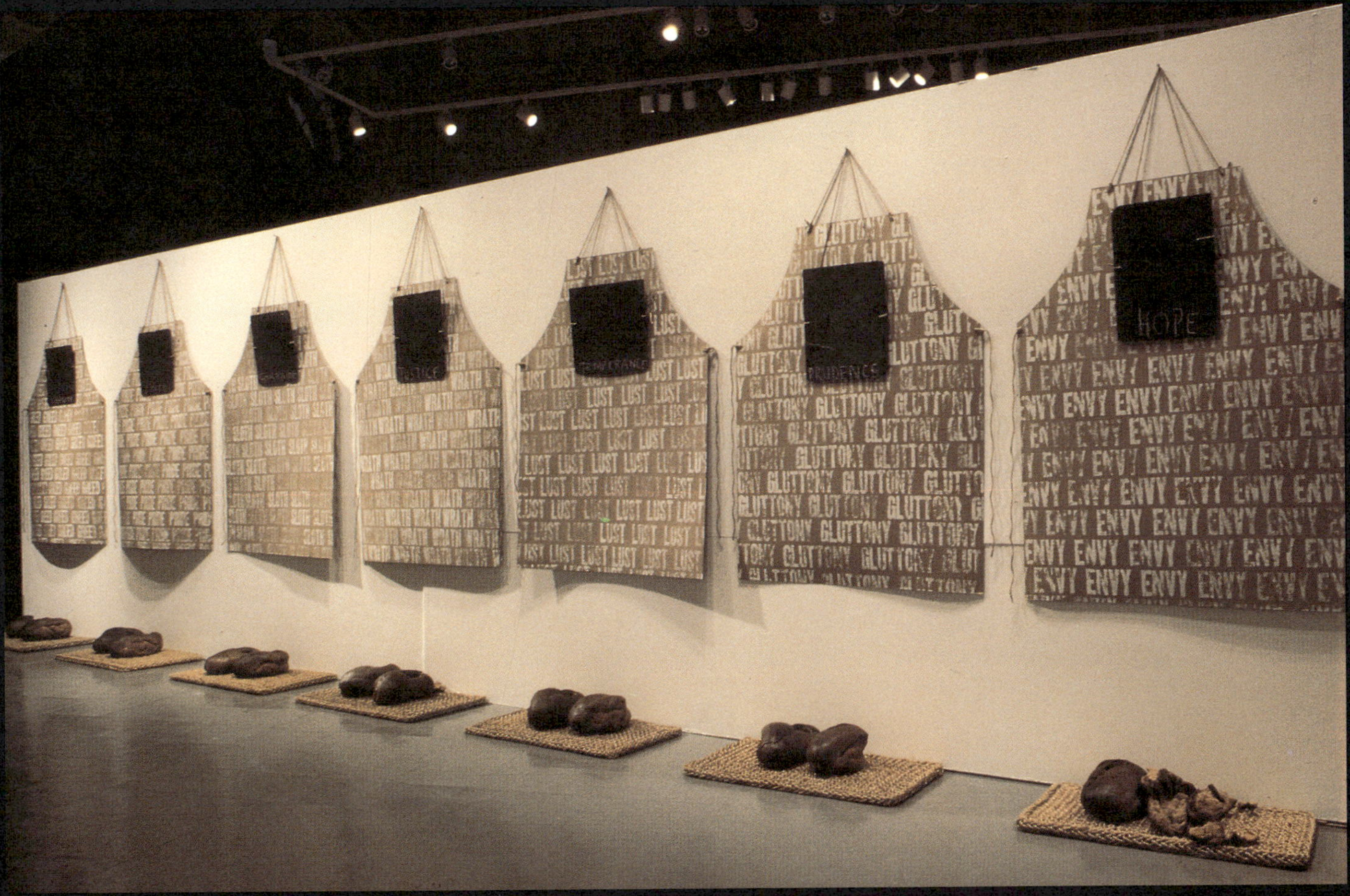
WRATH
LUST
PRUDENCE
GLUTTONY
HOPE
ENVY

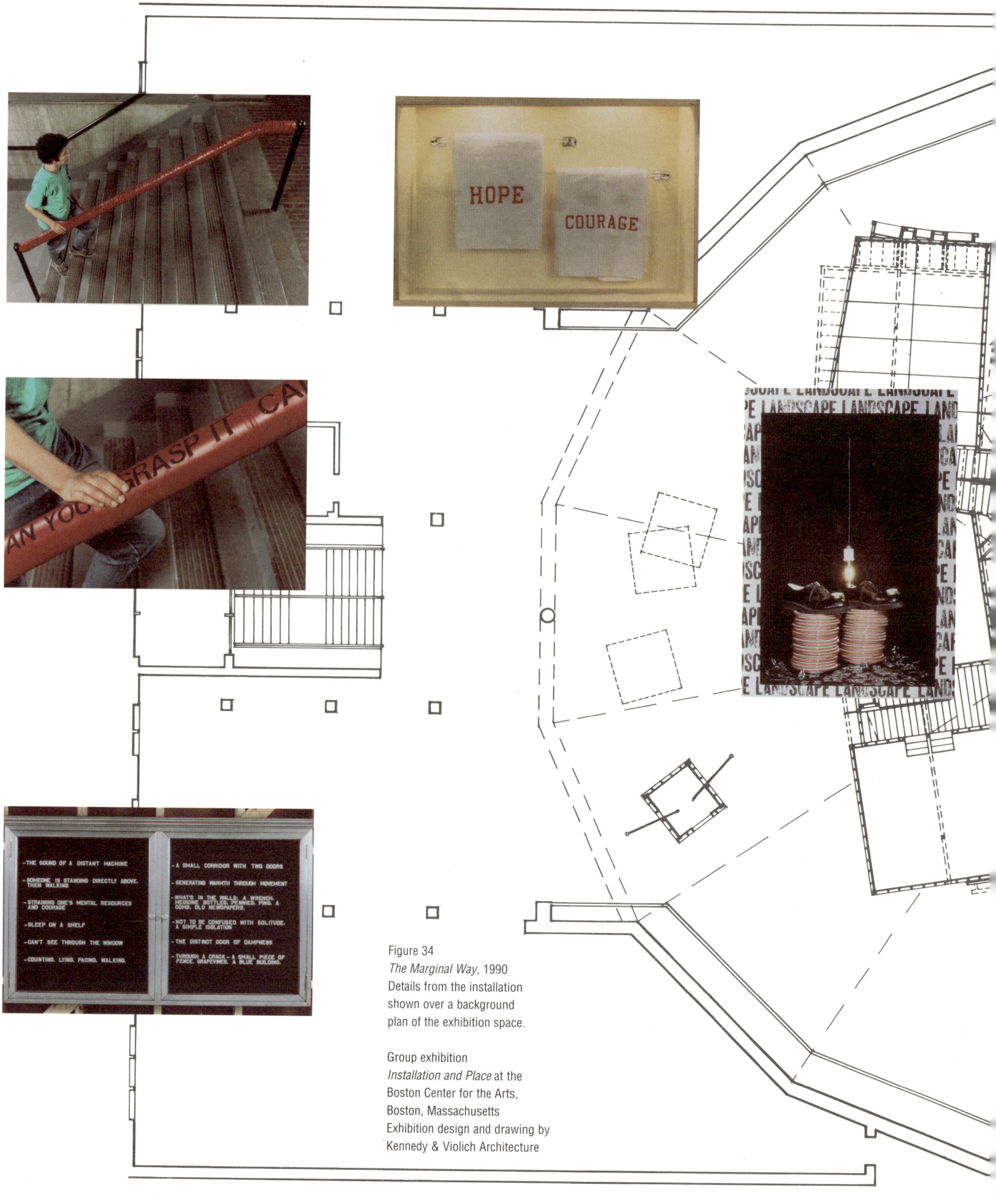

Figure 34
The Marginal Way, 1990
Details from the installation shown over a background plan of the exhibition space.

Group exhibition
Installation and Place at the Boston Center for the Arts, Boston, Massachusetts
Exhibition design and drawing by Kennedy & Violich Architecture

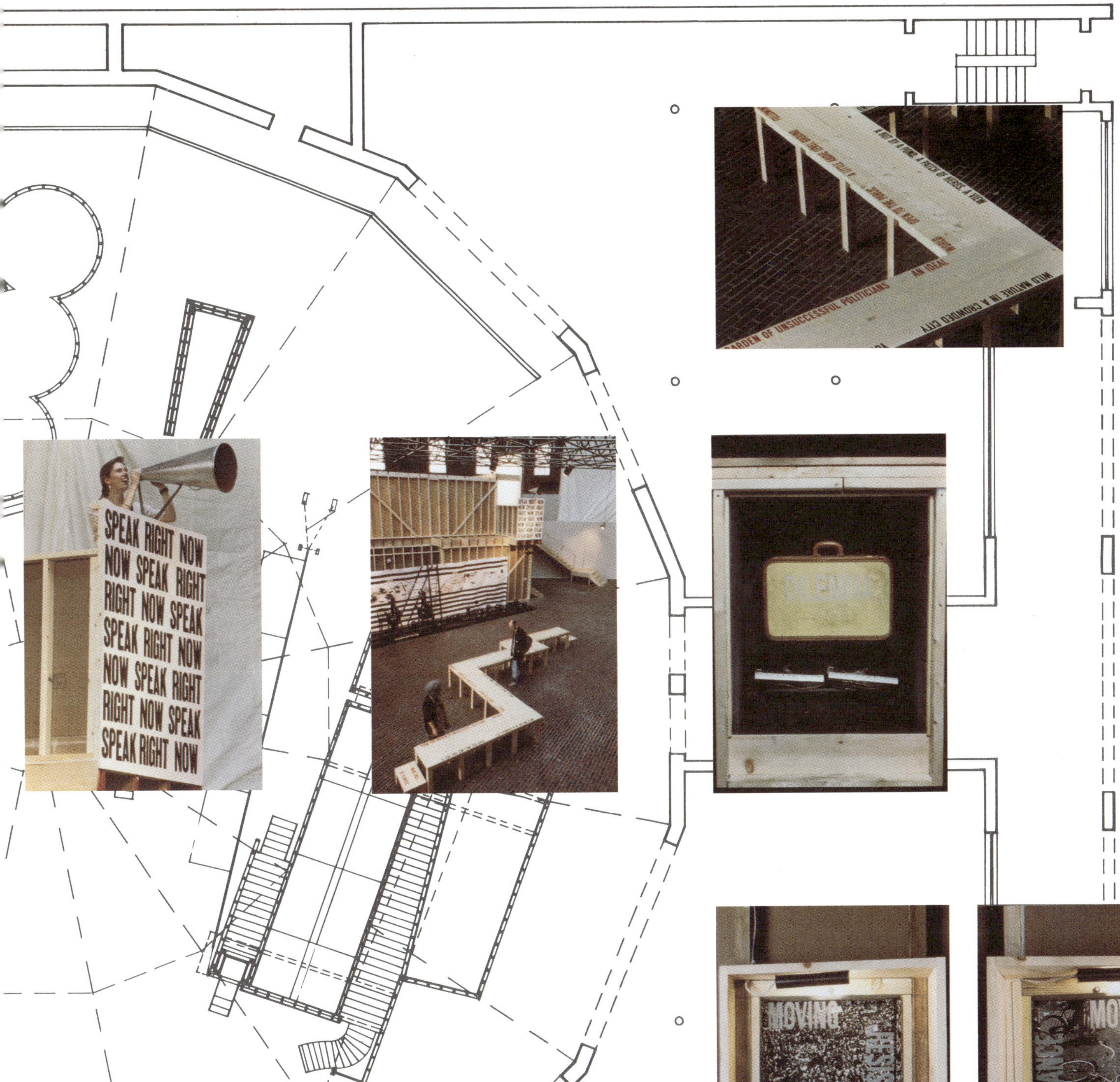

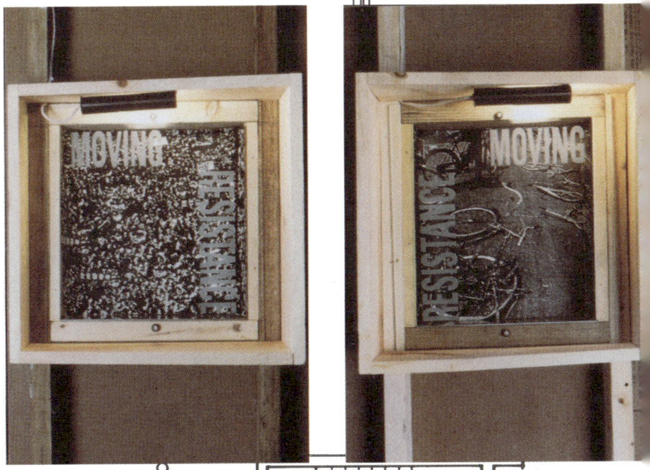

"The Marginal Way suggests a multi-level landscape within an architectural space. Moving through the exhibition as if on an exploratory journey, the viewer encounters a series of "trail-markers." The subtext of these markers reflects upon questions of personal location and the possibility of physical movement. As a grouping strategically sited within the architecture of the exhibition, these trail markers become the viewers' landmarks and mapping points."
— *Ellen Rothenberg*

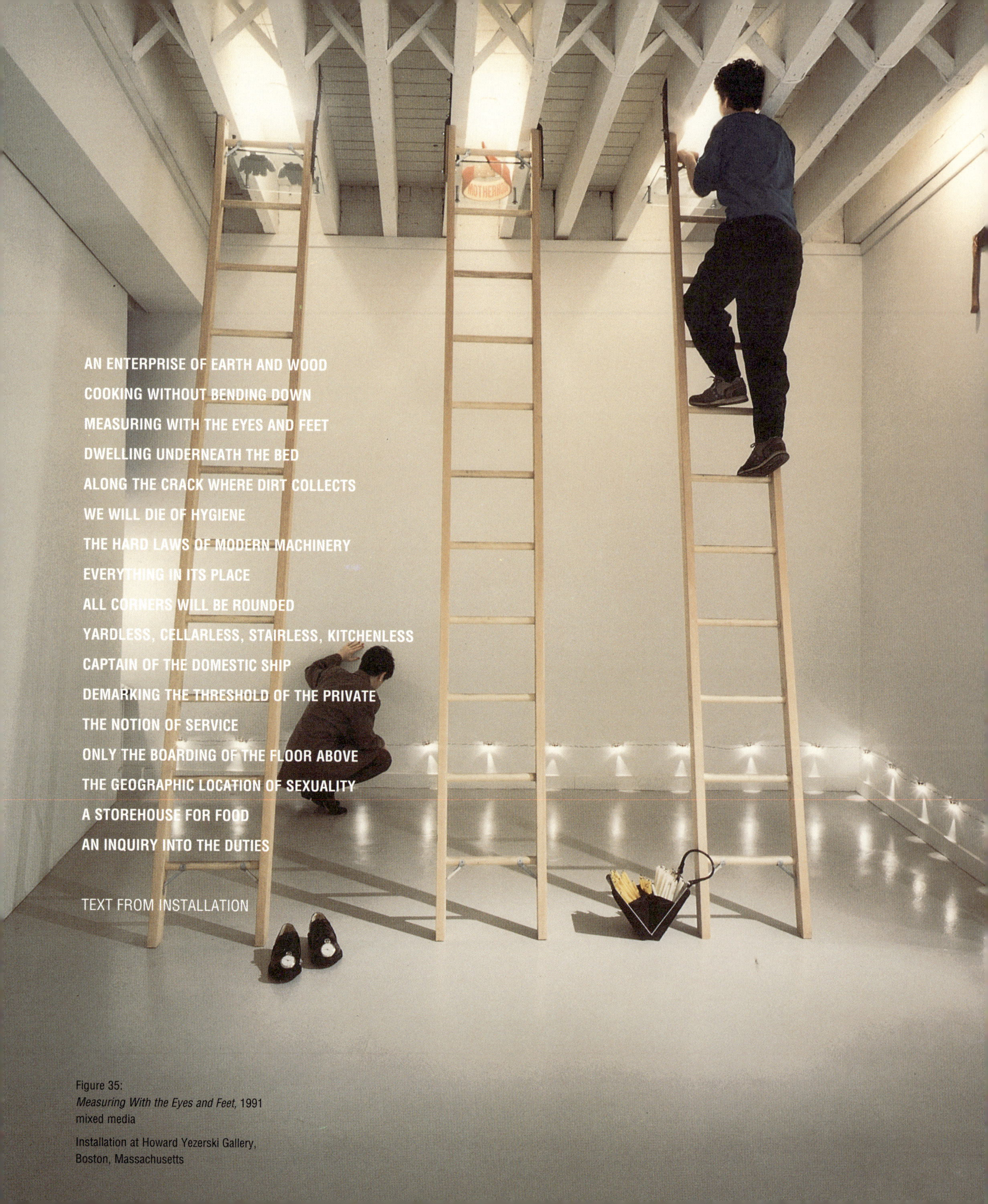

AN ENTERPRISE OF EARTH AND WOOD
COOKING WITHOUT BENDING DOWN
MEASURING WITH THE EYES AND FEET
DWELLING UNDERNEATH THE BED
ALONG THE CRACK WHERE DIRT COLLECTS
WE WILL DIE OF HYGIENE
THE HARD LAWS OF MODERN MACHINERY
EVERYTHING IN ITS PLACE
ALL CORNERS WILL BE ROUNDED
YARDLESS, CELLARLESS, STAIRLESS, KITCHENLESS
CAPTAIN OF THE DOMESTIC SHIP
DEMARKING THE THRESHOLD OF THE PRIVATE
THE NOTION OF SERVICE
ONLY THE BOARDING OF THE FLOOR ABOVE
THE GEOGRAPHIC LOCATION OF SEXUALITY
A STOREHOUSE FOR FOOD
AN INQUIRY INTO THE DUTIES

TEXT FROM INSTALLATION

Figure 35:
Measuring With the Eyes and Feet, 1991
mixed media

Installation at Howard Yezerski Gallery,
Boston, Massachusetts

Disjecta: observations, speculations and ruminations on Ellen Rothenberg's Anne Frank Project

by Lynne Cooke

1. "A Model of Experience: A Discussion on *A Model Childhood*", in *The Fourth Dimension: Interviews with Christa Wolf*, Verso, London & New York, 1988, pp.43, 56-57

"I would like to make it harder to forget.... I try to break through the purely rational communication of knowledge or experience.... It seems to me that where the past is concerned...we have filtered our emotions out too much. They are left standing alongside knowledge, but outside it; one is alone with them.... The one without the other, though, produces remarkably split personalities, as we can see around us....

I think that a lot that happens in the world is allowed to occur because we lack vision, because our powers of imagination are too weak to allow us to put ourselves in the position of the people to whom it is happening. But the smaller the world becomes through technology, the more important it becomes to develop the virtue of sympathy with what is alien to us.....[L]iterature, among other things, ought to do precisely this: exercise our imagination, develop our vision...so that contemporary history finds us capable of proper feelings and able to act according to our own judgment."[1]

It can be said of Ellen Rothenberg as of Christa Wolf, the renowned (East) German writer, that a moral code of artistic behavior rather than an aesthetics regulated by the senses informs her art. In Rothenberg's oeuvre, as in Wolf's, a number of abiding precepts govern each new project: the legacy of the past as it shapes the present; the contestatory operations of memory and amnesia; the social as well as moral responsibility integral to the role of the artist. Each artist invents novel modes of working partly because each views the standard art-forms as traditional male preserves. Thus Wolf has had recourse to other, non-literary forms—travelogue, diary, letter—in addition to fracturing those narrative unities particular to the traditional novel via the insertion of the voice of the author as both agent and commentator.

Rothenberg's forms are equally unconventional, spanning as they do the sculptural object, multiples, installation, placards, clothing, gift shop items, and performance. Sometimes she incorporates pre-existing objects, manipulating them marginally (*Guilt Erasers*,

Fig.39), sometimes she makes replicas (the cast combs); sometimes she makes new composites entities (*Footprints*, Fig.38) and sometimes she makes wholly symbolic constructs, as with the hair composed of strands of paper overprinted with the text of Anne Frank's diary (Fig.45).
The actual, the authentic, the copy, the facsimile, the surrogate....From issues of originality and duplication burgeon questions of truth and duplicity, plus a recognition of the ways that notions of truth are constantly open to slippage and redefinition depending as they do on the situation and context, the frame of reference. The vagaries of memory — the interventions of amnesia including the proclivity to hide and suppress what is uncomfortable — and the splitting of affectivity from intellectual knowledge are all brought under scrutiny. In both artists' work a preoccupation with the interplay of history and memory leads to a belief in subjective authenticity, inner truth in preference to mimesis, and verity over vraisemblance. By means of multiple perspectives, the elimination of a single authoritative viewpoint, and the eschewal of a unified linear "text," the viewer is brought to a self-conscious reflection on the processes of constructing meaning and imputing veracity. "Reminding, remembering and narrating are closely bound together, "Wolf has argued. "One reason for the emergence of narration, if we look at it historically, is that the members of society...needed to feel remembered, or to be reminded of their long past history. The recalling of history and stories in order to make the village, tribal, or national community aware of its own origin and development has always been a function of narration."[2] And she continued in terms that apply equally to Rothenberg's works where the apprehension of the various parts and components implies the weaving together of a composite multi-layered story, "In spite of all the other forms of media which have taken away from narration, this function of remembering and chronicling an aspect of that original meaning remains in our modern narrative, though admittedly other tasks have devolved upon it...." [3]

Although one artist is American and the other German, one Jewish and one not, they approach their underlying subjects in remarkably similar ways, testimony perhaps not only to the centrality and pertinency of their subject matter but to its place in contemporary collective memory.

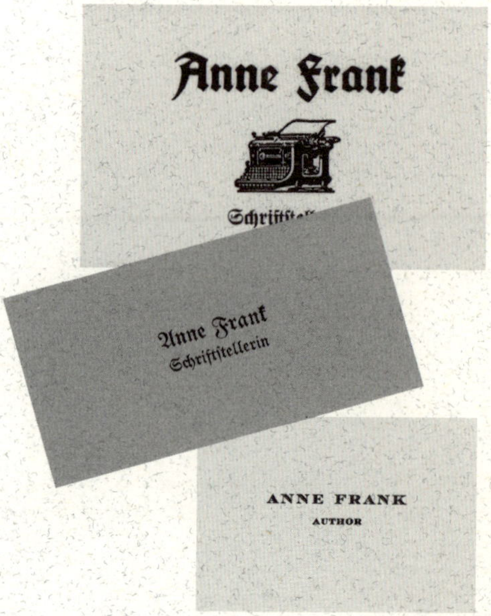

2. "The Origins of Narration: A Conversation with Jacqueline Grenz", in *The Fourth Dimension*, op.cit., p.127

3. ibid

Figure 36 (left and below):
Anne Frank Business Cards,
1991-2
assorted paper with letterpress printing, from the installation
A Probability Bordering on Certainty

Figure 37 (right): *Signage,* 1993
laser printed text and frames
6 in. x 8 in.
from the installation
A Probability Bordering on Certainty

Installation at
The Mary Ingraham Bunting Institute, Radcliffe College
Cambridge, Massachusetts
1993

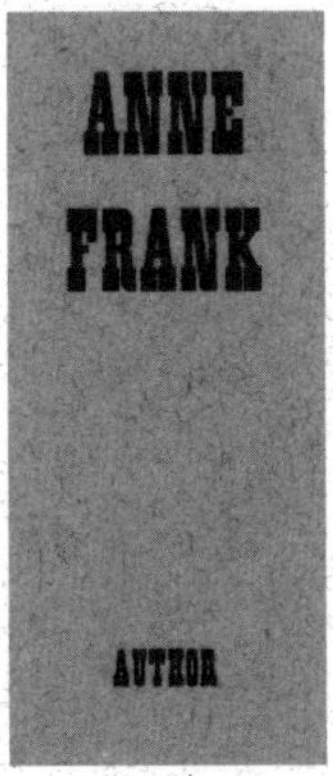

II.

The reluctance of many of Rothenberg's contemporaries, as of those older, to rekindle memories of the Holocaust, and to move beyond a routine recognition to a felt engagement with its legacies, is arguably comparable to the unwillingness that Wolf's generation in East Germany displayed to resurrecting their relationship to their fascist past, to childhoods lived through the years of Nationalism Socialism, and to the question of the relationship between that past and the socialist present (notwithstanding premature declarations of denazification purportedly achieved through re-education). In her longstanding fascination with the life and diary of Anne Frank, Rothenberg has found a subject of intrinsic import that can also operate as a vehicle for examining certain larger issues. After spending almost two years in hiding with her family in Amsterdam, the period during which she wrote her celebrated diary, this Jewish teenager died in the German concentration camp of Bergen-Belsen in 1945. That both her life and her art have been the subject of literary machinations, misrepresentations, and betrayals since they first came to public attention in the late forties is crucial to Rothenberg's project.

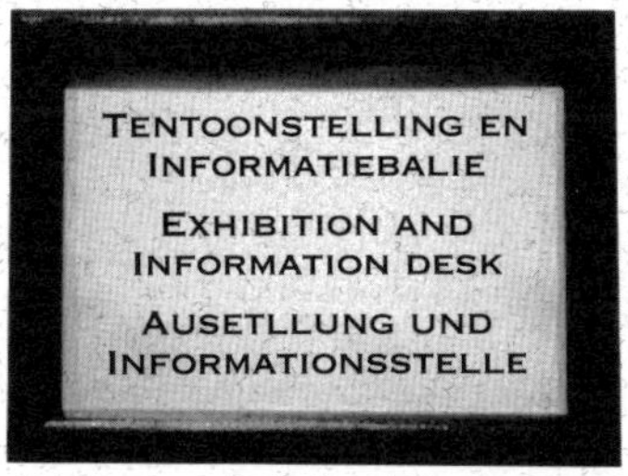

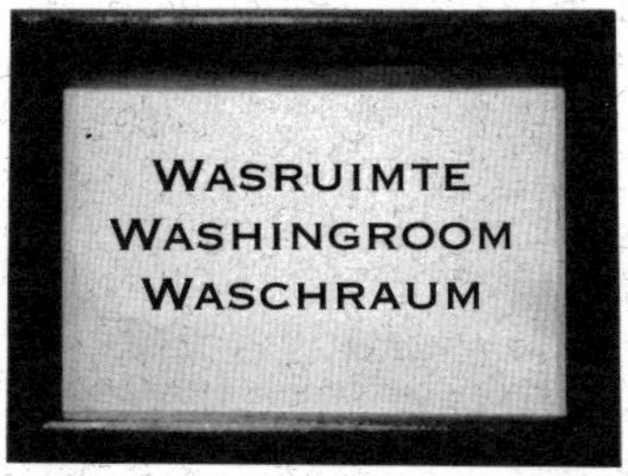

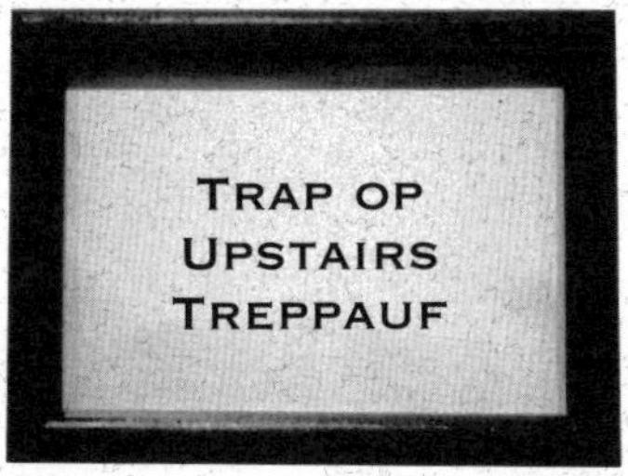

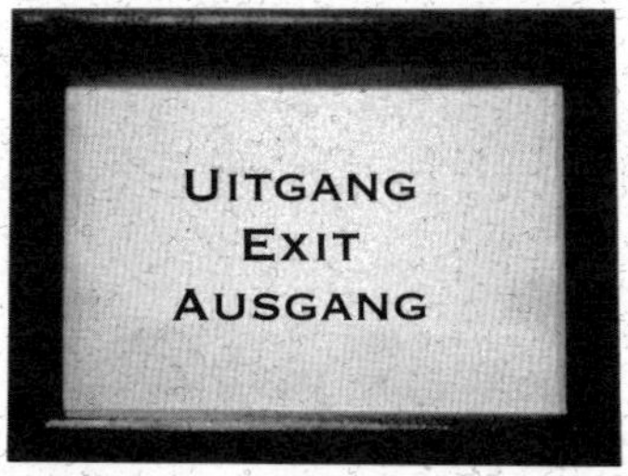

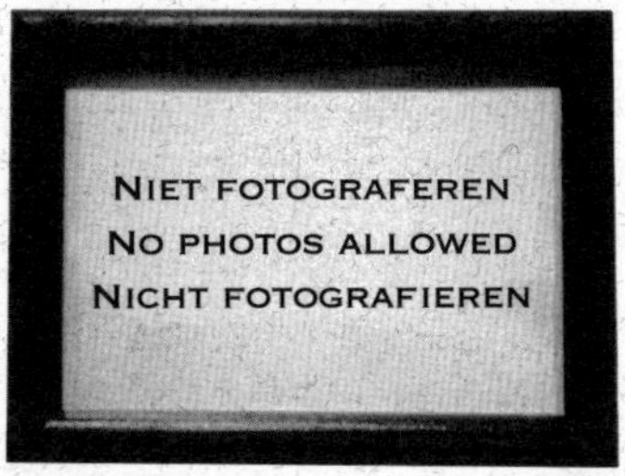

The best known name, aside from that of Hitler, to be associated with the Second World War, Frank's has come to represent unshakable belief in human goodness, and exemplary courage in the face of oppression. As the fame of her life's tale resounded so the interpretations of it mutated. Typically, and in the United States as much as in West Germany, her plight was increasingly detached from the specific circumstances, the socio-historical and cultural context in which she lived, to be transformed into a generalized account of courage in the face of unspecified evil; a stress, that is, on the ostensible universality of her predicament rather than on the details of Jewish cultural life that contributed centrally to her very sense of self. The goal was thus an optimistic, inspiriting message rather than the recounting of a tragedy. In this process of presenting the diary as literature rather than as an historical document, editorial deletions plus certain acts of censorship occurred which were the work of publishers in different countries tailoring the original manuscripts to the perceived needs of their audiences, as well as of writers adapting her daily entries to the demands of different media, notably the cinema and theatre. For example, several sections in which her burgeoning sexuality (menstruation) occupied her thoughts, as well as a number of dismissive comments on German nationals, were deleted. Complicity, collusion and censorship together helped transform this complex living being into a factoid, a media construction of enormous if increasingly cliched currency. In recent years various types of revisionist history have sought to extract the original text from the mass of later encrustations and omissions. At the same time neo-fascist cadres have questioned the authenticity of the diary as an historical document in an attempt to discredit not only Frank's memory but accounts of the horrors perpetrated by Nazism in general. And, in 1981, an international commission asked to verify the authenticity of the diary reached a verdict of "probability bordering on certainty."[4] Their conclusion raises the question that, given the necessity of dealing with the inevitable lacunae and lapses in information due to the passage of time, what is the measure of truth? And does — or can — inner truth override literal veracity?

Whether conducted in the service of canonizing saints, or alternatively, of unmasking and defrocking legendary heroes, research into, and examination of, mythic personages is part of the proper and necessary work of historians, scholars, and other intellectuals. In inserting some of this information into the visual field Rothenberg uses techniques of overlay, juxtaposition, and self-cancelling, together with the refusal to privilege one position or viewpoint over another, in order to divest her presentation of hierarchies and authoritative perspectives. In this way her work not only provokes enquiry in place of passive consumption but instills an awareness that the act of interpreting is a reading-in — a tying together of threads, and an interpolation, and hence as far removed from a detached scrutiny of so-called facts as from a self-confirming recognition of supposed truisms. Any closure of meaning becomes an arbitrary intervention by the viewer in the act of apprehending information. To take one example, a recent work (Fig.36) is comprised of an array of calling cards with different designs and typefaces, and even alternative languages which nonetheless preserve the same text, intimating

4. see David Barnouw, "Attacks on the Authenticity of the Diary," in *The Diary of Anne Frank: The Critical Edition*, prepared by The Netherlands State Institute for War Documentation, Doubleday, New York, 1989, pp.84-103. The examining body was the State Forensic Science Laboratory of the Dutch Ministry of Justice.

something of the subtly but tellingly diverse ways Frank has been presented, appropriated and defined. But here, as elsewhere in Rothenberg's art, it is the silences and absences which are equally eloquent: there is no card in Hebrew, for example. In place of a unified, coherent entity Frank's identity is revealed to be the sum of multiple subjectivities.

III.

Museums, especially those which mark the birthplaces of celebrated figures or the exploits of famous personages, are necessarily involved with the contingencies and accidents of history. For it is such events which transform commonplace objects into legendary exemplar. In such institutions the incidental and the significant, the banal and the unique, are woven together into dioramas whose raison d'être is the recreation of the actual but irrecoverable past. Although their displays depend primarily on relics, on both objects and artifacts from the past, documentary material may be incorporated to round out the presentation, counterpointing the creation of affective experience via illusory means with the conveyance of information by didactic methods. Further polluting this mix are such ancillary museological appurtenances as signage, and safety and sanitary equipment.

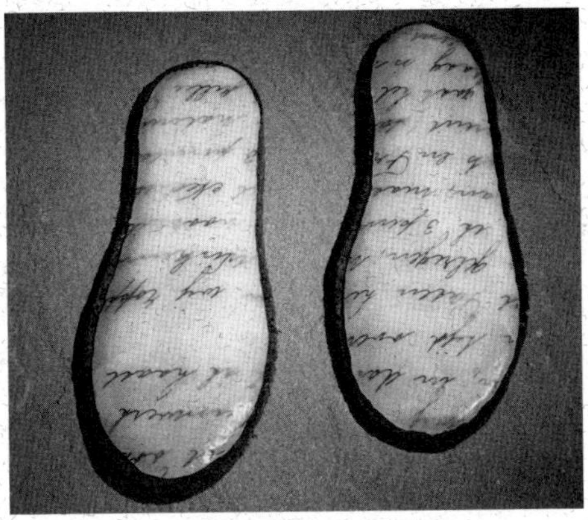

Figure 38, *Footprints,* 1991
printed text on rice paper, wax and felt,
11 3/8 in. long x 4 1/4 in.wide x 5/8 in.
Collection of Charlene Engelhard

To the degree that the historical museum, like the diorama, habitat group or period room proposes immersion in an authentic experience rather than a representation of it, it risks blurring the boundary between illusion and reality. For when objects are transformed from fragments to components in a free-floating totality their realm becomes an imaginary or metaphorical one, one whose existence lies within the frame of the aesthetic or the fantastical.

In her exhibitions in both galleries and museums Rothenberg comports with various methodologies of display, though installation remains her preferred approach to presentation. To date those of her works based around the theme of Anne Frank have been incorporated into

5. Susan Stewart, *On Longing: Narratives of the Miniature, the Gigantic, the Souvenir, the Collection*, The Johns Hopkins University Press, Baltimore, 1984, p.163

constructed environments. These room-like structures envelop the viewer in a space whose parameters, character and ambiance in the manner of the diorama conceal and shield all evidence of the nature of the actual site, the white walled neutralized enclosure. Rothenberg's contextualising is designed to create the semblance of an authentic experience, yet one that is constantly rendered self-critical and reflexive. In the context of her installations the various works offer themselves as original, unique artifacts while simultaneously subverting their claim to authenticity.

In historical displays, actual relics risk becoming neutralized by the museum experience, and so of losing affectivity as the museum extracts them from the continuous present to place them in the stasis of a supposedly timeless presentation — which is, in fact, the perpetual past. Alternatively, they may be in danger of being subverted into the spectacular and exotic. Rothenberg astutely negotiates these different possibilities in a number of ways, not least by treating her artifacts as mnemonic devices, as signposts which chart a labyrinthine course through the installation and thereby through the mind of the viewer. In this her installations are reminiscent of the Renaissance memory theatre, an architectural edifice whose elements served as allegorical repositories for storing in orderly sequence items of knowledge that might otherwise have remained irrecoverably trapped in the dusty unmapped byways of the scholar's mental universe. They recall, too, Gaston Bachelard's notion of the mind as a building whose secret passages, attics and cellars are all depositories for different types of experience which can be only revisited by touring its circuitous corridors.

If photography and related reproductive techniques today constitute the most ubiquitous and, often, preferred, means to recording history they do not fully answer the question of how to deal with the past if history is to be more than a repository of material artifacts and indexical images, if it is also to embody memory — collective and personal memory. Artifacts in the guise of iconic images, fetishes and even souvenirs, play a crucial role in enhancing the impact of the document by recharging the antennae of recumbent memory. Cultural critic Susan Stewart contends that "the boundary between collection and fetishism is mediated by classification and display in tension with accumulation and secrecy."[5] Rothenberg's displays breach these perimeters to partake of both the apparently objective and taxonomic, and the acquisitive and sequestered. Strategically forcing the viewer to shift between these competing modes of organization, her work participates in its own disclosure. In so doing her installations discourse on the mechanisms and conventions by which museological display operates. Their strength lies in their ability to do this without fully forfeiting the emotional rewards that museum display customarily seeks to generate as it endeavors to recapture memory by recreating history. ■

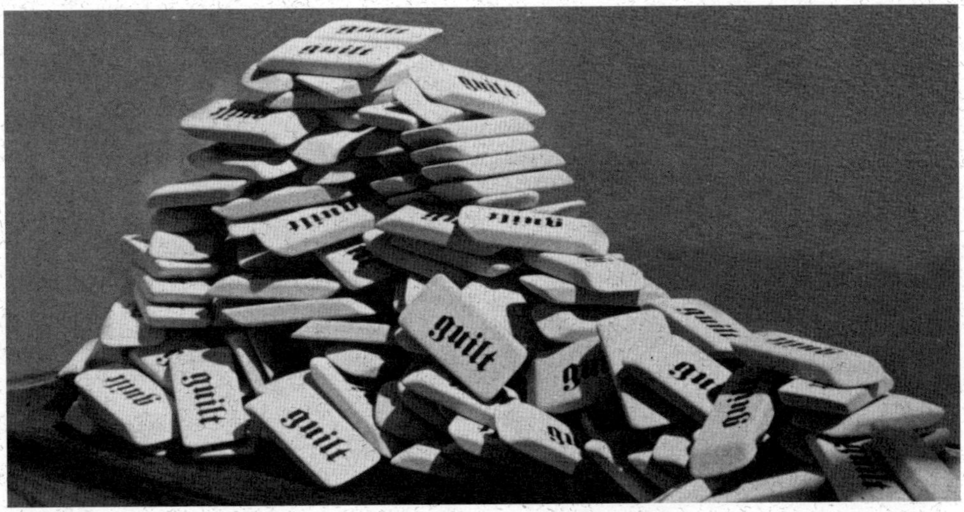

Figure 39: *Guilt Erasers,* 1993
printed text on rubber, unlimited edition
from the installation
A Probability Bordering on Certainty

Installation at
The Mary Ingraham Bunting Institute
Radcliffe College
Cambridge, Massachusetts

CODA:

This essay was written before the author became aware of Christa Wolf's relations with the Stasi during the years 1959-62, as documented in the Inoffizielle Mitarbeiter (Informal Collaborators) files. How this material should be assessed, and what are its implications for any reading of her work, are deeply complex issues. In respect of this essay the interpretations offered still seem to stand. In the larger arena, it is important to beware not only in relation to Wolf but to the many artists and others newly implicated by the opening of these files of the danger of making the Stasi the adjudicators of truth. As Wolf herself points out: "This perverse mountain of files has turned into a kind of negative grail, to which one makes a pilgrimage in order to experience truth, judgment or absolution. Nothing better, really, could have happened to the Stasi after the fact: banal, narrow-minded file administrators and information fetishists turn state's evidence and receive once again, in some cases now truly for the first time, the power to judge the fates of human beings." quoted in Peter Demetz, "The High Cost of a Dream," *The New York Times Book Review*, April 4, 1993.

Figure 40: installation view,
A Probability Bordering on Certainty,
1993
Background: *Handwriting Analysis*.
Foreground: *Das Wesentliche*

Installation at
The Mary Ingraham Bunting Institute
Radcliffe College
Cambridge, Massachusetts

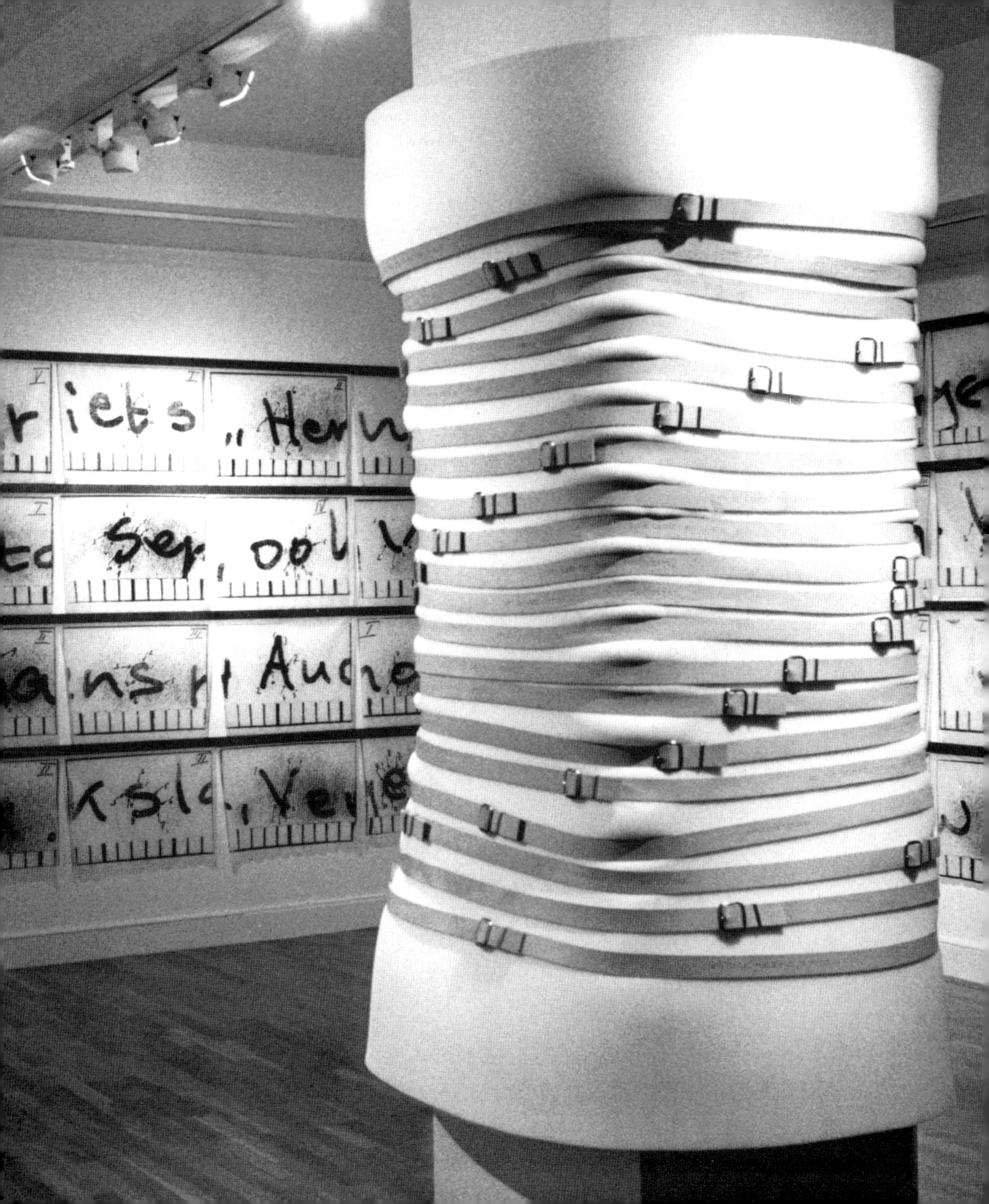

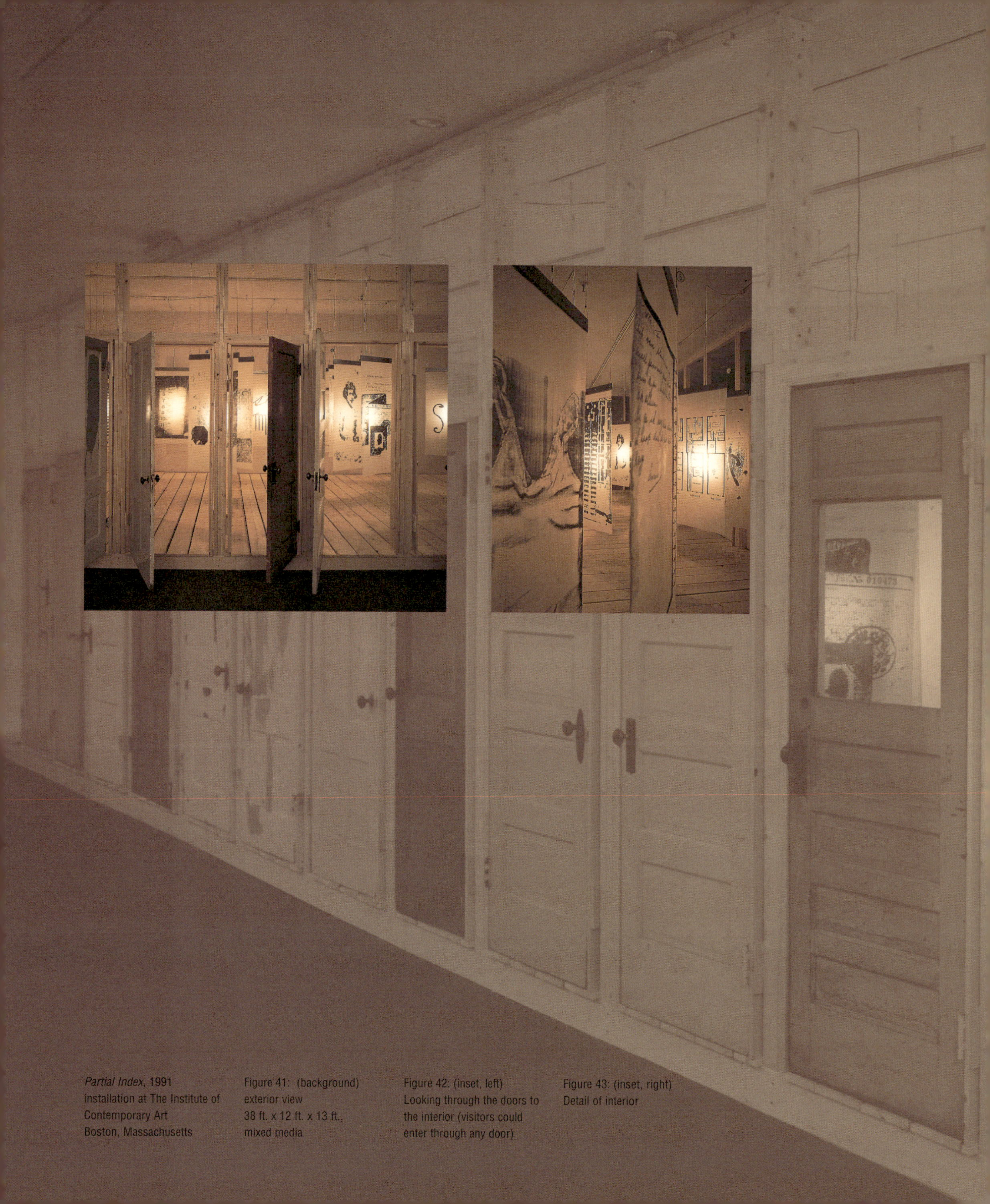

Partial Index, 1991
installation at The Institute of Contemporary Art
Boston, Massachusetts

Figure 41: (background)
exterior view
38 ft. x 12 ft. x 13 ft.,
mixed media

Figure 42: (inset, left)
Looking through the doors to the interior (visitors could enter through any door)

Figure 43: (inset, right)
Detail of interior

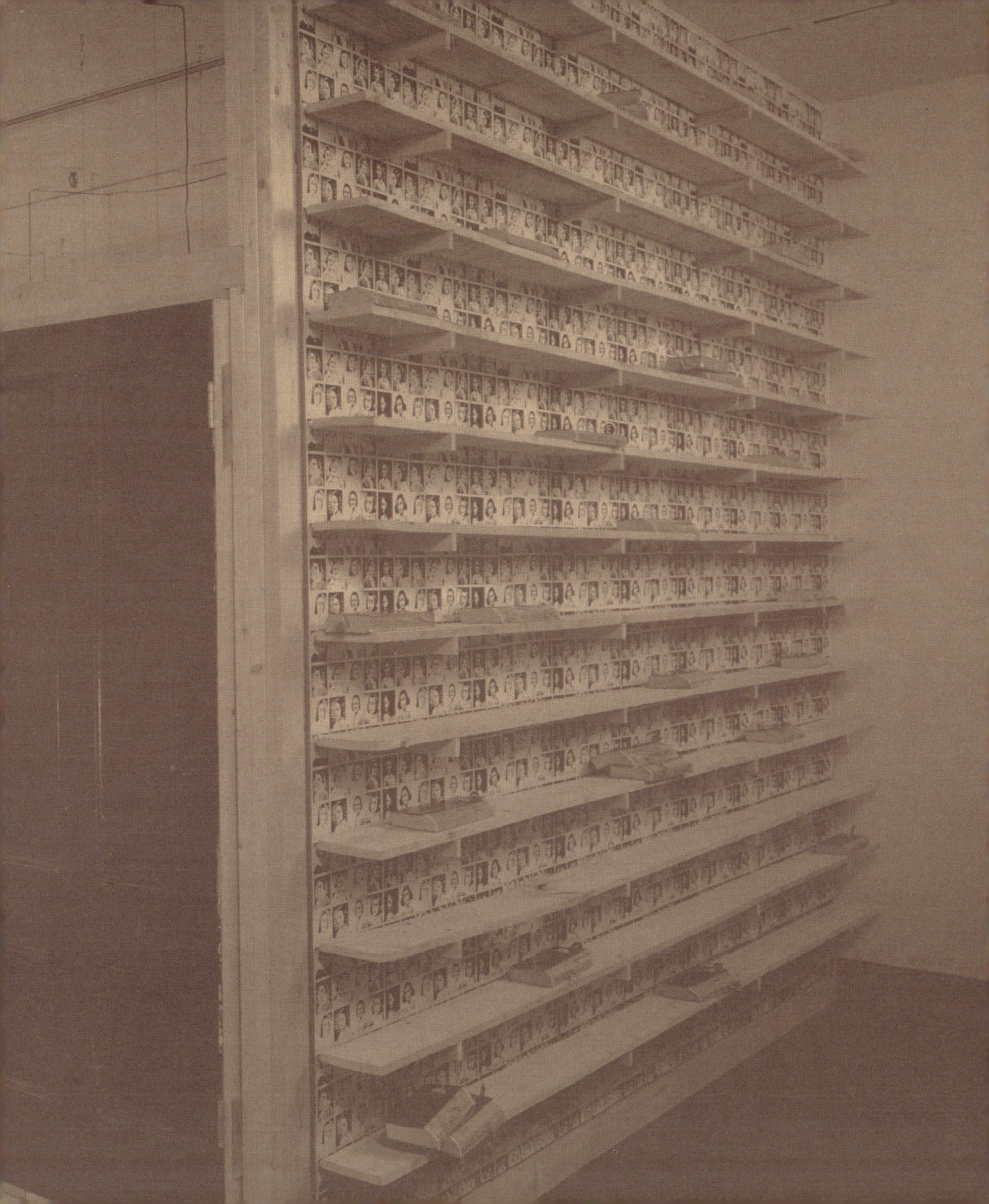

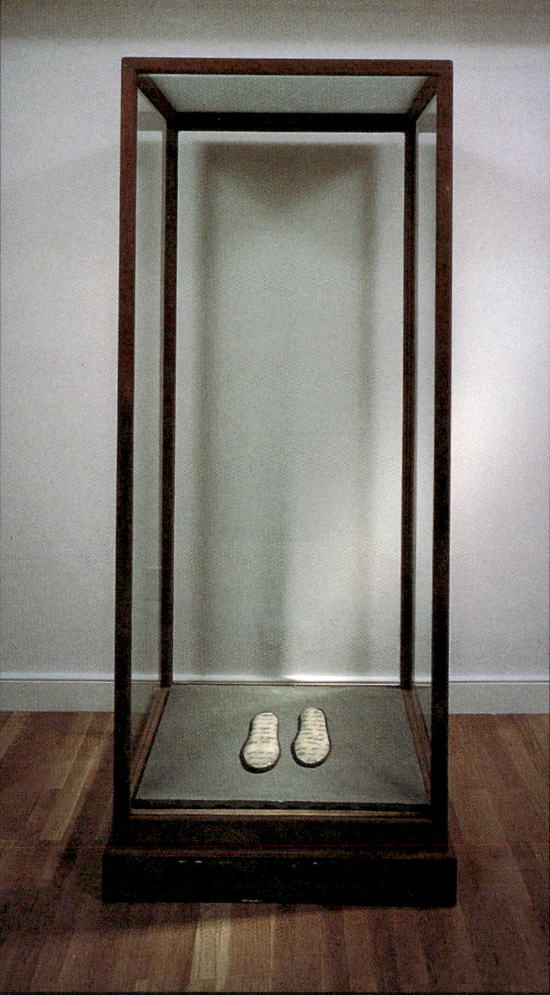

Figure 44: *Footprints*
from *A Probability Bordering on Certainty*, 1993

Installation at
The Mary Ingraham Bunting Institute Radcliffe College
Cambridge, Massachusetts

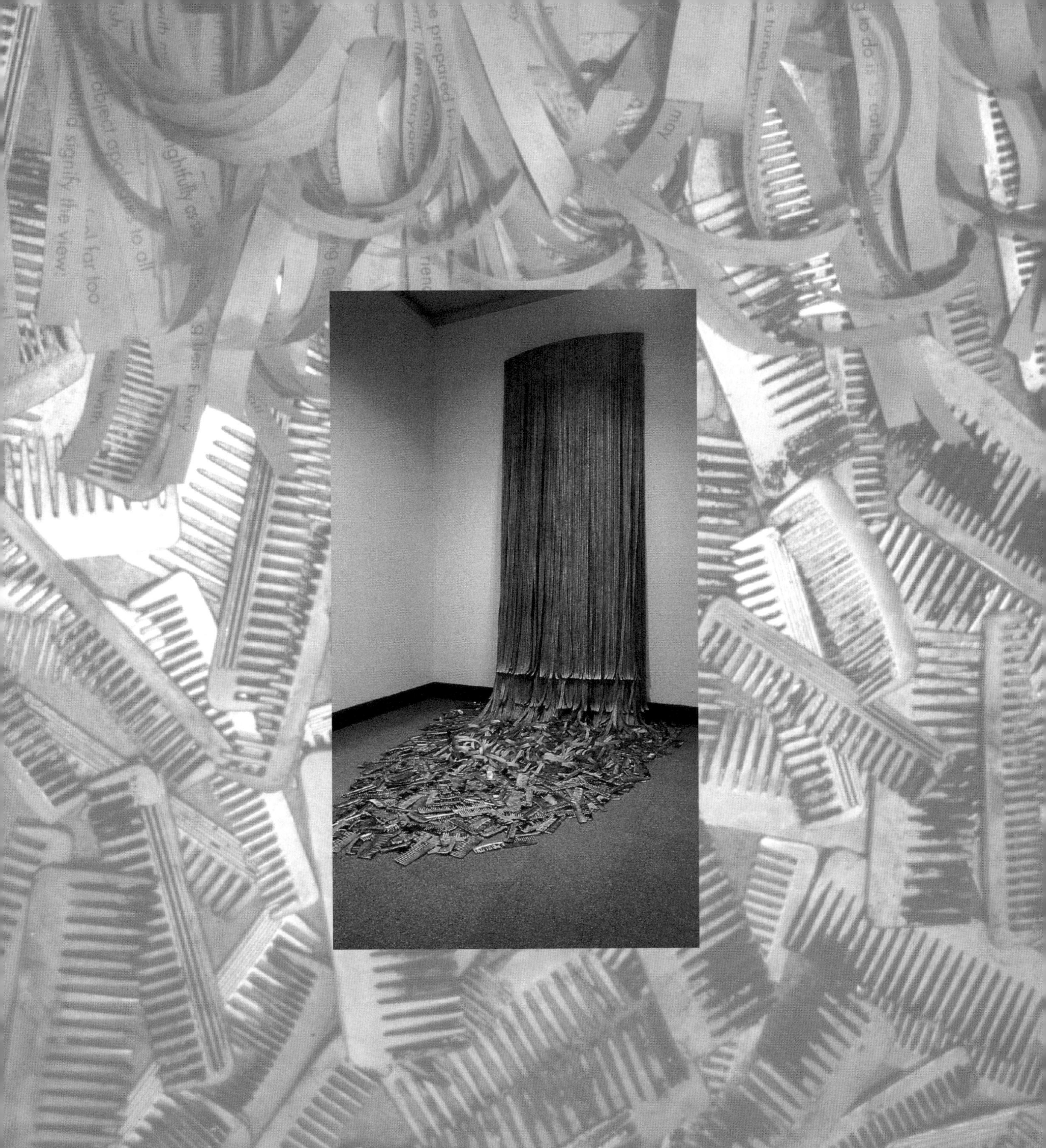

Figure 45: *The Combing Shawl, 1993*
text of the *Diary of Anne Frank* printed on vellum, graphite, aluminum and steel brackets, 350 combs cast in various metals
from *A Probability Bordering on Certainty,* 1993

Installation at University Art Museum, University of California
Santa Barbara, California

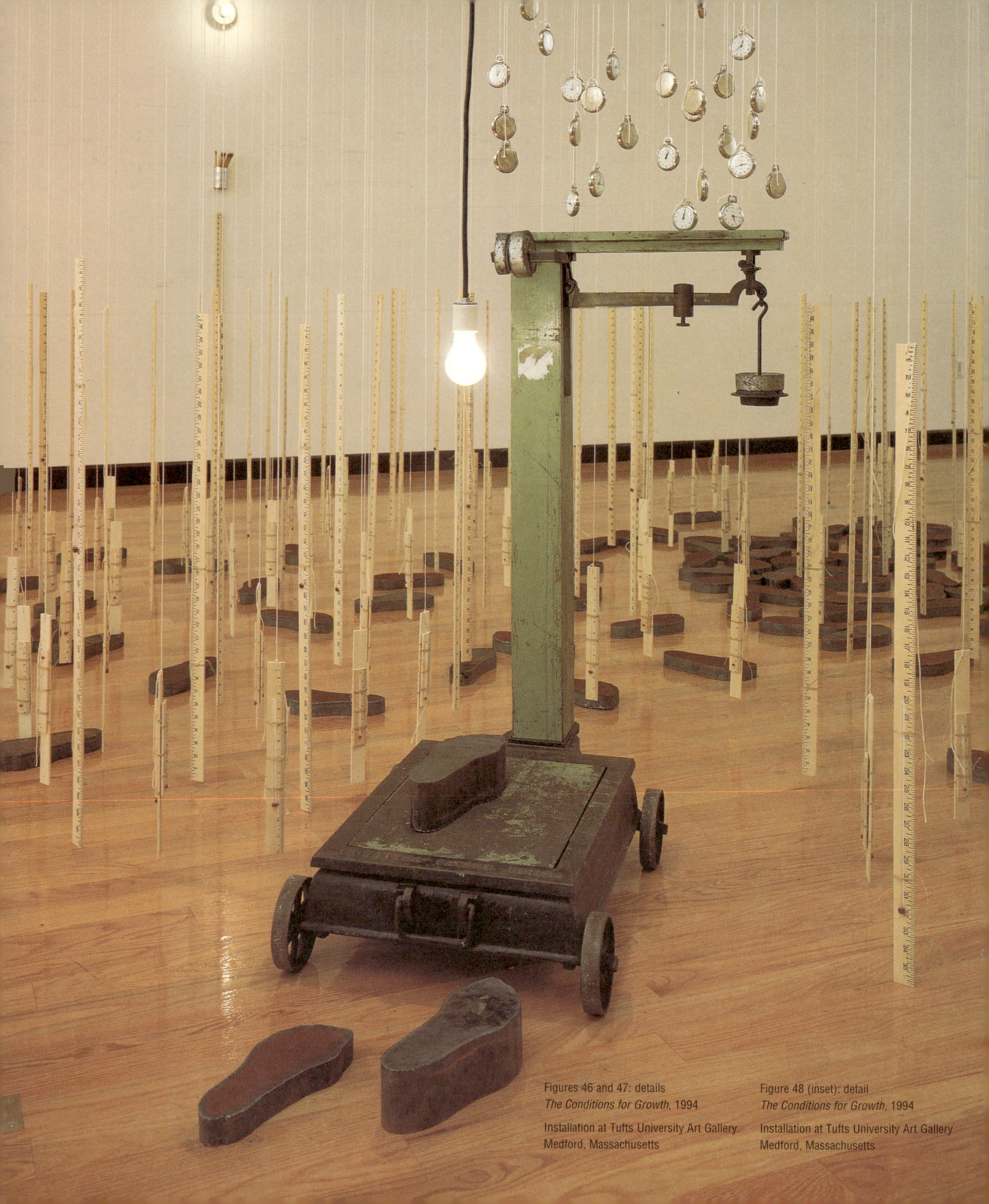

Figures 46 and 47: details
The Conditions for Growth, 1994
Installation at Tufts University Art Gallery
Medford, Massachusetts

Figure 48 (inset): detail
The Conditions for Growth, 1994
Installation at Tufts University Art Gallery
Medford, Massachusetts

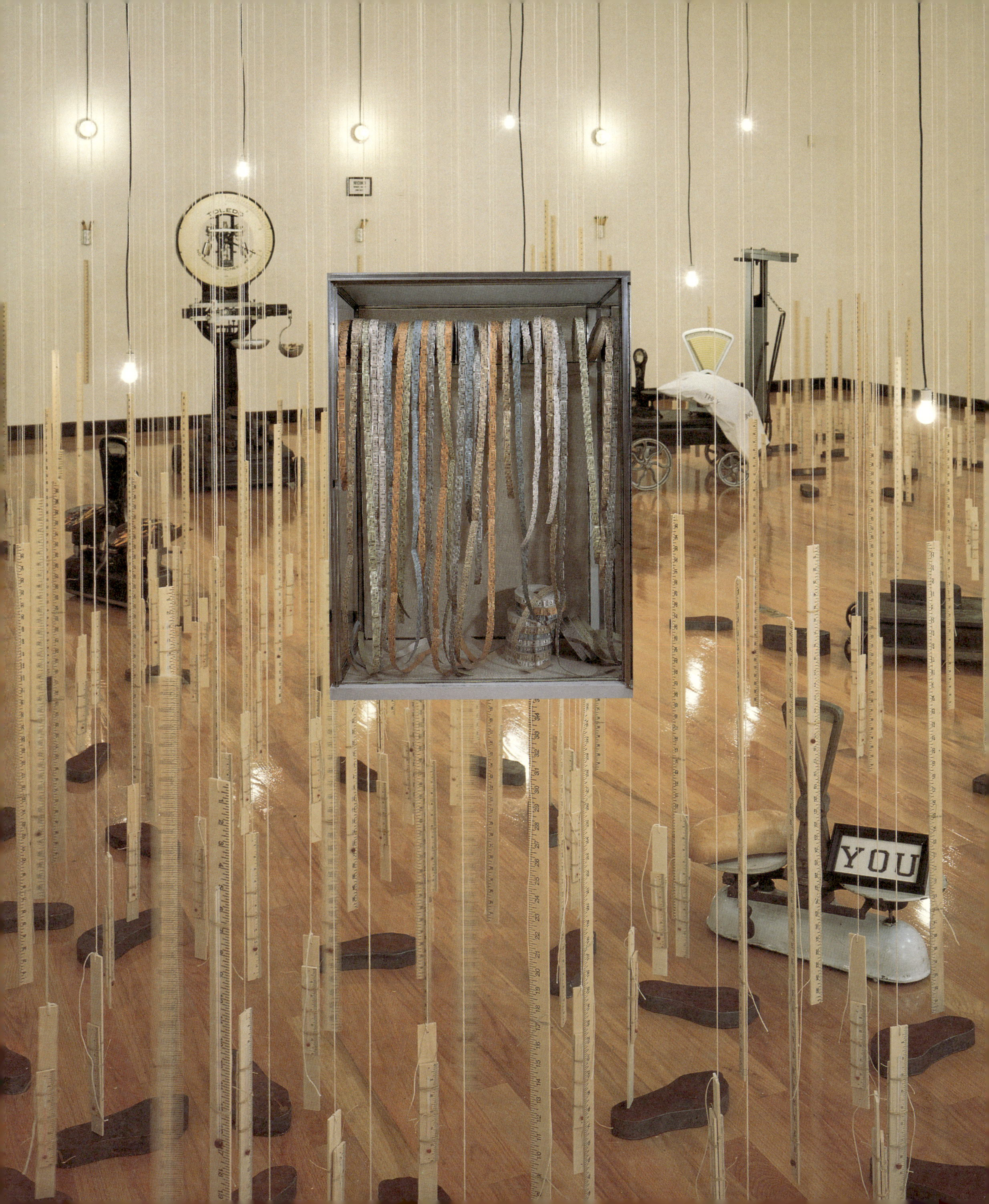
TOLEDO
YOU

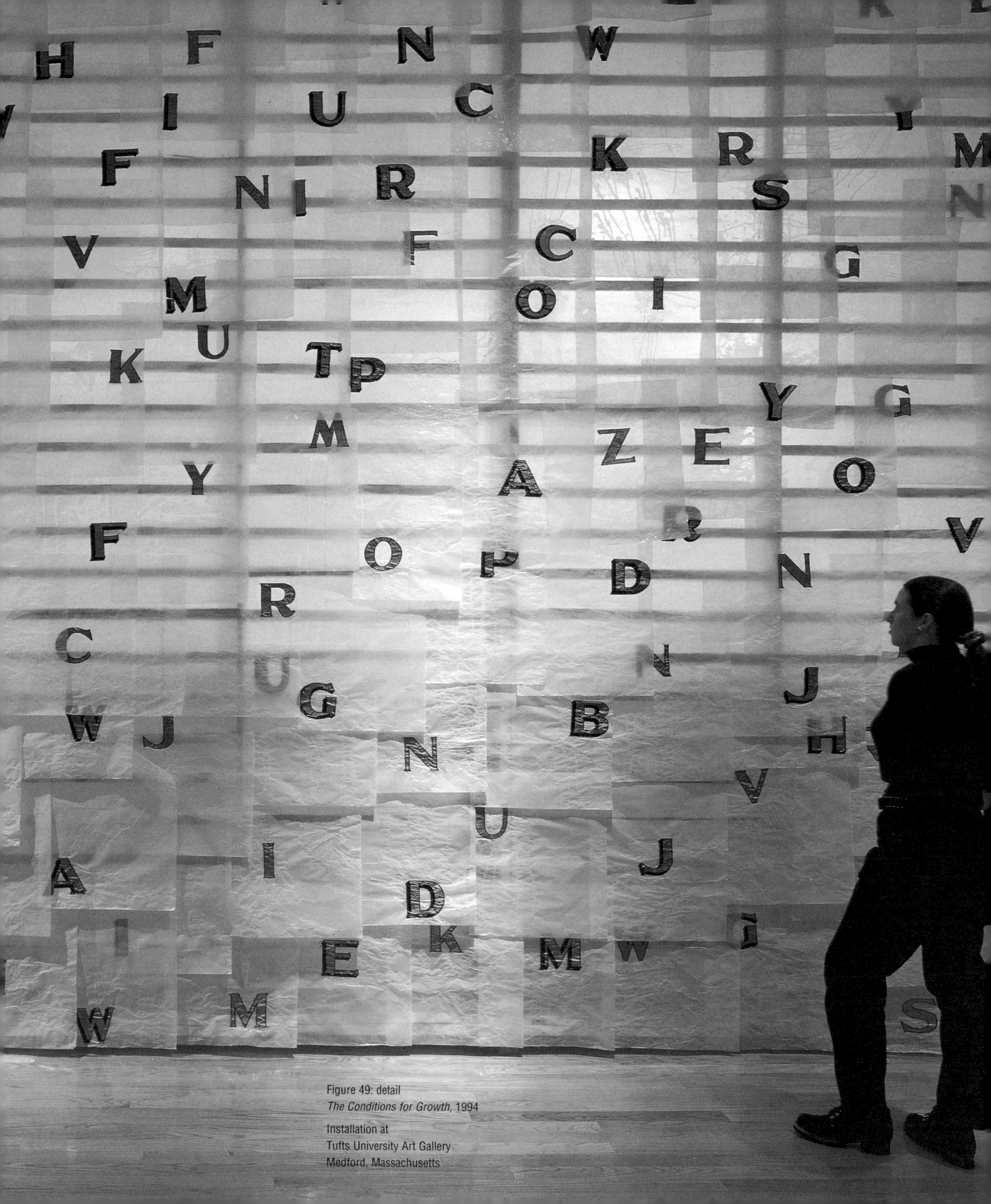

Figure 49: detail
The Conditions for Growth, 1994

Installation at
Tufts University Art Gallery
Medford, Massachusetts

The Conditions for Growth

Whitney Chadwick

The Holocaust continues to haunt the twentieth century in part because, in the words of Alvin Rosenfeld, "...what cannot be satisfactorily represented can be neither fully comprehended in the present nor securely retained in memory for the future."[1] To an artist, motivated by the need to apprehend, and to embody meaning within the material, an event the magnitude of which defies both comprehension and representation calls into question the creative act itself. Ellen Rothenberg's *The Anne Frank Project*, an ambitious three-part installation begun in 1990, explores both the parameters of this historical narrative—through its artifacts and documents, its silences and absences, its uncertainties and ambiguities—and the moral responsibility of the artist to bear witness to history.

The Anne Frank Project is not a documentary about the young Jewish girl whose two years of hiding in Nazi occupied Amsterdam ended with her death at the Bergen Belsen concentration camp in 1944. Its subject is not the facts of history, whatever they may be, but its successive representations and permutations as Rothenberg first experienced them through reading the *Critical Edition* of the diary. It is history viewed through the lens of the Anne Frank story, as it was recuperated and rewritten, reinvented and transformed. It is history understood as systems of knowledge and information rather than events. And it is Rothenberg's insertion of herself—female, Jewish, vanguard artist—into a history which effectively silenced the voices of Jewish women and modern artists.

Partial Index (Fig.41), the first of Rothenberg's three installations, opened in 1991 at Boston's Institute of Contemporary Art. Reproductions of "documents" from the life and times of Anne Frank were interspersed with "false artifacts" in a large architectonic wooden "room" organized to suggest a giant filing cabinet or rudimentary computer. Fabricated images (a radio, a monogrammed handkerchief, a girl's undershirt) called into question the ability of any artifact to "stand for" reality, and spoke to the difficulty of representing the past through its survivals in the present. Hanging panels of text, written by the adolescent Anne but omitted from the published version of the diary by her father, and images taken from a forensic handwriting analysis conducted to "prove" the diary's authenticity in the face of challenges by neo-Nazis were printed on fragile sheets of rice paper and sealed with beeswax and paraffin. Like ghostly traces of missing realities, they called into question the "evidence" that forms our history, while at the same time blurring the distinctions between truth and fiction, the real and the represented.

The second part of the project, titled *A Probability Bordering on Certainty* (selections from which were first installed at the Bunting Institute at Radcliffe College (Fig.40), where Rothenberg was a fellow, in May 1993), was based on research undertaken by the artist during a nine month stay in Germany in 1991. Visits to the National Forensic Science Laboratory in Rijswik, and the Anne Frank Museum in Amsterdam with its "reconstructed"

1. "Anne Frank—And Us: Finding the Right Words," *Reconstruction* vol. 2., no. 2 (1993), p. 86.

secret annexe, led her to confront her own assumptions about the documentary nature of her project, and to explore the difference between imagining and experiencing history. The heart of the installation was composed of fragments of text taken from the handwriting analysis. Enlarged until they "read" as gestural marks rather than linguistic signs, framed by the measured markings of the forensic scale, and photocopied onto thin sheets of silk tissue, they covered the walls with a fragile "skin." This porous and translucent membrane, transmitting an ethereal light as it quivered in response to the movements of spectators in the gallery, also evoked the permeable barriers that sustain life in all organisms, whether single cells or complex bodies. The scientists' conclusion of authenticity—"a probability bordering on certainty"—served as a powerful metaphor for the uncertainties of both history and science.

Rothenberg also used different categories of objects: both actual historical artifacts from Anne Frank's life, and objects from daily life which were available both during the 1930s and today (among them enamel signs, certain hand tools and work clothes) as a matrix within which to explore the ways that our experience of history is mediated by the conventions of its display. What relationship can a facsimile environment have to the original, she asks? How do we reconstruct history from the fragment? What role does museum display play in how we understand the past?

Since Rothenberg undertook *The Anne Frank Project* in 1990, the history which she has chosen to address has undergone its own successive transformations. The enormous popular appeal of recent events like the openings of the Holocaust Museum in Washington, D.C., and Stephen Spielberg's feature film *Schindler's List* point to more contemporary reinscriptions of the imagery of the Holocaust in the popular imagination. The Bitburg Cemetery that President Ronald Reagan insisted on visiting over the protests of his own advisors as well as representatives of many Jewish groups, was an actual place: the site of the burial of SS soldiers who had participated in the burning alive of over 600 French women and children at Oradour sur Glan. The opening of the Holocaust Museum on the Mall in Washington, alongside memorials to the country's founding fathers and its twenty year war in Vietnam, signals a loosening of the ties that once bound the images and artifacts of the Holocaust to the specifics of place and time.[2] Once liberated, they often assume new meanings as they circulate across geographical and historical boundaries. The much-heralded premier of *Schindler's List* further reconstituted this imagery in the public imagination, linking it to institutions and forms of entertainment and popular culture, much as the 1955 Broadway play *The Diary of Anne Frank* had done for an earlier generation.

The Conditions for Growth, Part III of *The Anne Frank Project*, which opened at the Tufts University Art Gallery at the beginning of 1994, reframes Rothenberg's earlier investigation of history within a more studied interrogation of the politics of collecting, display, and cultural identity. As the gallery space itself begins to function as a locale of spatial and temporal indicators, objects and images imply metaphors and narratives within a fictional space that suggests a vast airy warehouse. The presence of a wall of industrial steel shelving filled with numbered cardboard boxes holding objects like light bulbs and rolls of twine underscores this association (Fig.50).

2. for further discussion of this phenomenon, see Thomas Laqueur, "The Holocaust Museum," *The Threepenny Review*, no. 56 (Winter 1994), pp. 30-32

Unlike the Dada or Surrealist Found Object, however, the objects which Rothenberg has chosen (or in some cases manufactured) are not just occasions for reverie or for psychic dislocation. Instead they point in multiple directions: on the one hand, toward Germany's history as an industrial nation and, more obliquely perhaps, toward the Holocaust's deployment of industrial technologies and human labor on a mass scale; on the other, toward the elusive ways that personal and cultural identities are formed through the arbitrary systems of meaning and value that we assign to the manufacture and consumption of objects, both personal and cultural.

Entering this fictive space, the spectator passes by a "wall" made up of sheets of translucent glassine (Fig.49), each bearing a single pressed gold letter. These decals (originally manufactured for a now obsolete system of commercial window signage) were transferred using water, a medium that wrinkles and activates the surface. They were then sealed with a thin coating of wax. Unlike the handwriting analysis that figured so prominently in the previous installation, and that reduced cursive script to abstract marks, the wall of letters forces the viewer to confront the enigma of linguistic building blocks that are at once concrete (printed letters) and ephemeral (without meaningful linkages). An alphabet is not yet language and this disjunction serves as a fitting introduction to the installation as a whole.

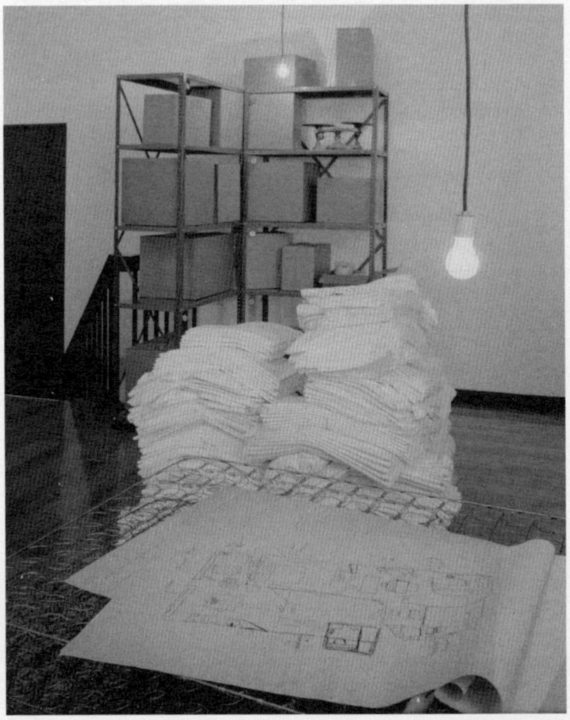

Figure 50:
detail
The Conditions for Growth, 1994

Installation at
Tufts University
Art Gallery
Medford,
Massachusetts

Once inside the larger gallery space the viewer confronts the problematics of an historical consciousness produced through a selection of "artifacts." The display of these bits of "evidence" in glass vitrines and free-standing piles underscores the capriciousness of collecting, the arbitrary nature of the processes through which we seek out and/or claim that which we choose to recuperate, and the fact that the harder we work to "document" the past through its physical survivals the more elusive its meanings become.

Beyond the wall of letters, the interior of the gallery space is broken into two areas by the placement of large groups of objects. In one, an assortment of glass display cases mounted on rolling dollies emphasizes the provisional nature of the "history" presented here (Fig.51). In another, some twenty five hundred wooden rulers and yardsticks hanging on strings from a frame attached to the ceiling create a "forest" of signs (Figs.46-47). Glass thermometers bound to each ruler imply a reference to the human body, drawing the viewer into a heightened awareness of the interplay of presence and absence within a space both mental and physical.

A scattering of bare lightbulbs hanging low from black electrical cords illuminates the space around the rulers. On the floor thick steel footprints (originally torch-cut using a pre-World War II industrial technology) crisscross the fragile field of suspended measuring devices. Nearby a small cluster of pocket watches hanging from strings tick audibly. Large old-fashioned industrial scales scattered throughout the installation "weigh" still more collections of objects: pencils, glass thermometers, more footprints, a pillow cover embroidered with the words "Where Have They Gone?" A loaf of bread and a small framed piece of wool bearing the monogrammed word "You" balance each other on the bed of a large scale, incorporating the human element into the weighing and measuring of raw materials. At intervals along the walls that frame this section of the installation, visitors are offered pencils and encouraged to inscribe their own physical measurements on the white wall (Fig.53).

Defined by rulers and scales, weights and measures, a physical space is marked and quantified, its contents sorted and weighed, but at the same time rendered fluid, ephemeral and allusive. Rothenberg's point of departure was another set of measurements: the inscriptions that appeared on the wall of the Frank family's "secret annexe" on the Prinzengracht canal, markings that measured the heights of the three children hidden within—Anne, Peter and Margot—and that survived their subsequent imprisonment and death. Those marks survived as poignant signs of the ways that humans under siege often seek to normalize life in the face of external threat, to locate sanity in the ordinary and the everyday. It is a process that can be read even today in newspaper and television images from Belfast to Sarajevo.

At the same time, the simple and apparently "objective" act of measuring and testing, quantifying and assessing, assumes terrifying dimensions when placed within the context of Nazi Germany's deployment of statistical and scientific "evidence" in support of its to register social groups. As part of that history, millions of individuals were labeled "degenerate" in order to be eliminated, reduced to names scratched on concentration camp walls, and fragments like the piles of hair clippings and gold fillings recovered at Auschwitz and other sites. Millions more were measured against a mythic ideal of the "pure German" produced, circulated, and reinforced through the visual images of the Third Reich's massive propaganda campaigns, their identities "proved" by another kind of scientific weighing and measuring. Yet within a different German history, that of post-war economic recovery, precise measurement became an economic indicator, an index of production capacity and technological might within an international community of industrial powers. The ends to which empirical knowledge is put are ideologically formed. Often they encompass choices as disparate as whether to commit resources to curing disease or producing weapons of mass destruction. In framing questions of choice, *The Conditions for Growth* functions as a critical practice within the discourse of contemporary art. Contesting Enlightenment assumptions about scientific objectivity, Rothenberg's installation draws attention to the practice of science as another cultural institution structured by the political, social, and economic values of the dominant culture.

If the recuperation of history informs Rothenberg's project, and I think it does, the question of history itself—and its relationship to the objects through which we approach it—remains open-ended.

Figure 51: detail
The Conditions for Growth, 1994

Installation at
Tufts University Art Gallery
Medford, Massachusetts

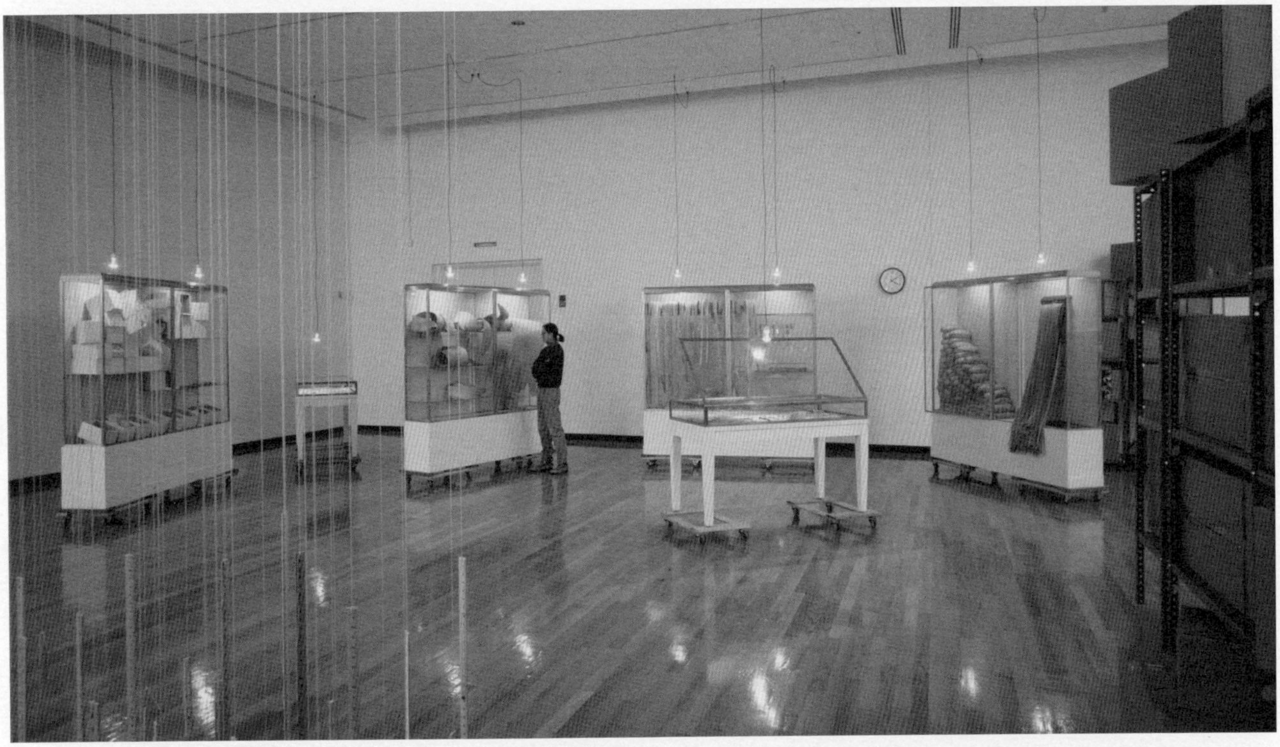

Like all visitors to museums, whether of art or natural history, we are presented with salvaged objects, fragments of cultural life and natural history which conjure up whole worlds of possibilities. And we are in turn forced to question their sources, the reasons for their selection, their value and meaning. Obsession, whether triggered by the evidence of sheer numbers (the hanging rulers, for example) or by the unspoken desire of collectors everywhere to possess the world, forms a disturbing leitmotif as the installation's focus shifts from counting and measuring to collecting and displaying. As anthropologist James Clifford has pointed out, citing Baudrillard as well as the work of contemporary cultural anthropologists from Susan Stewart to Daniel Defert, collecting and display are crucial processes of Western identity formation:

> Gathered artifacts—whether they find their way into curio cabinets, private living rooms, museums of ethnography, folklore, or fine art—function within a developing capitalist 'system of objects'. By virtue of this system a world of *value* is created and a meaningful deployment and circulation of artifacts maintained. For Baudrillard collected objects create a structured environment that substitutes its own temporality for the 'real time' of historical and productive processes....[3]

In fact, the "artifacts" that Rothenberg has selected (or in some cases produced) for our visual consumption range widely across the cultural landscape. Some refer us to the specifics of Anne Frank's personal

3. James Clifford, "On Collecting Art and Culture." in the *Predicament of Culture: Twentieth-Century Ethnography, Literature, and Art*. Cambridge and London: Harvard University Press, 1988, p. 220.

history, and to items through which she was once known. Strips of paper printed with text from the original Diary stream like hair from "Scalp," a manufactured reference to "The Combing Shawl" included in the previous installation. There it signified the protective garment recovered from the secret annex after the Dutch Secret Police had cleared it, all that remained of Anne Frank's physical body. References to that body, and the adolescent girl's fantasies and projections of womanhood, appear on a collection of white kid gloves of differing lengths and styles spread out in a waist-high display case (Fig.52). All of them have been altered in some way: sutured with red thread as if they bore surgical wounds; printed with the titles of fables, short stories, and reminiscences written by the young girl ("Eve's Dream," "Fear," "Dreams of Movie Stardom"), stamped with images of red lice that recall the conditions under which she lived out her final imprisonment and death from typhus, a disease carried by lice.

Other artifacts (including loaves of bread and rolls of tickets (Fig.48) derived from ration books and printed in Dutch, German and English with the words "brood," "vlesch," "Drink," "Eat," etc.) refer to social systems of survival, privilege, and admission common during the 1930s, and in some cases still in evidence today. The recurring image of bread points both to the centuries old staple of the north European diet and to the conditions of near starvation endemic in the camps. Multiples of snapshots of inexpensive and widely available consumer goods (from metal hair rollers and tampons to toys and scales) have the look and feel of dated objects, but are actually images of products from the former East Germany. They recall the ways that historical memory is formed by everyday objects and simple rituals, as well as by cataclysmic events.

In another display case, five tanned hides, patterns of dates stamped on their surfaces with library stamps, lie in rolls on shelves. The largest of them, stamped with the dates of entries in Anne Frank's diary, bears mute witness to the Third Reich's use of skin as a decorative material, its denial of the individuality and integrity of the human body, and its deployment of the body itself as an amalgam of usable parts.

If we were to see the objects that comprise Rothenberg's installation in another context, as part of a display at Auschwitz or Sachsenhausen for example, they might take on other kinds of meaning. In the spaces of the art gallery, they become part of the bricolage of the museum and we become witnesses, not only to history, but also to the ways that objects are transformed into art. We read these artifacts, whether found or fabricated, in relation to those other objects—paintings, sculptures, drawings—that circulate within spaces such as this. And we confront the ways that the preservation and display of objects is tied up with the cultural and nationalist politics that produce our sense of who we are, both individually and collectively.

Rothenberg's collections also recall Nazi acquisitions and display policies: the looting and warehousing of art treasures in the salt mines of Austria; the proposed (but unrealized) Museum of the Extinct Race in Prague with its collections of everyday items. They offer evidence not only of the Nazi's desire to lay claim to the cultural history of the West, but also of their eagerness to use it as the raw material out of which to produce a cultural identity for the "new Germany." "When we celebrated the laying of the cornerstone for this building four years ago," Hitler noted at the opening ceremony of a lavish new museum (the *Haus der Deutschen Kunst*) in Munich in 1937, "we were all aware that we had to lay not only the cornerstone for a new home but also the foundations for a new and genuine German art."[4] Why this object and not that, Rothenberg seems to ask? And whose history is it anyway?

The representation of cultural identity, once primarily the province of anthropology, has increasingly become part of the discourses of art and art history. The issue was taken up first by artists of color forced to confront the cultural politics of canon formation, and the ways that definitions of mainstream are secured in relation to that which is marginalized (by differences of gender, race, ethnicity and/or sexuality). It has become the focus of others involved in the history of Diaspora, including those of Jewish heritage. Elaine Reichek's recent exhibition at The Jewish Museum in New York, *A Postcolonial Kinderhood*, and Deborah Kass's photographic series "The Jewish Jackies" and "My Elvis" (1992) (which include investigations of the imagery of Barbra Streisand) both address the cultural formation of Jewish identity in North America. And they do so by appropriating images and objects, and by subverting the meanings assigned to visual images by the dominant culture. *Conditions For Growth* also functions as a record of an artist's process, an archive of the objects collected by Rothenberg over the years she worked on *The Anne Frank Project*. It reinserts the Jewish woman artist into a history from which she was not only silenced, but often physically eliminated. In so doing, it demands that we move beyond emotional identifications with the story of Anne Frank, and pose tougher questions about our compliance with systems of acquisition and valuation.

The images and objects that mediate our relationship to the past form the basis for much of Rothenberg's powerful recent work. She demands that history be acknowledged as the social project that it is. She demands that voices silenced—whether through state intervention and coercion, or through social ideologies that naturalize assumptions about human, behavior, gender and race, be restored. In short, Rothenberg's project demands nothing less than that we examine our own assumptions about how our various identities are produced and circulated. ■

4. Cited in Stephanie Barron, et al, *"Degenerate Art:" The Fate of the Avant-Garde in Nazi Germany*. Exhibition catalogue (Los Angeles Los Angeles County Museum of Art, 1991) p. 18.

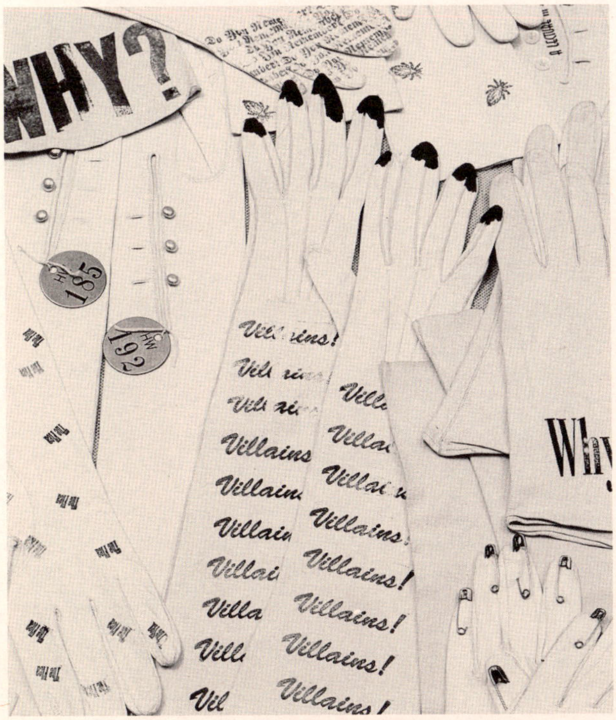

Figure 52:
detail
The Conditions for Growth, 1994
Installation at Tufts University Art Gallery
Medford, Massachusetts

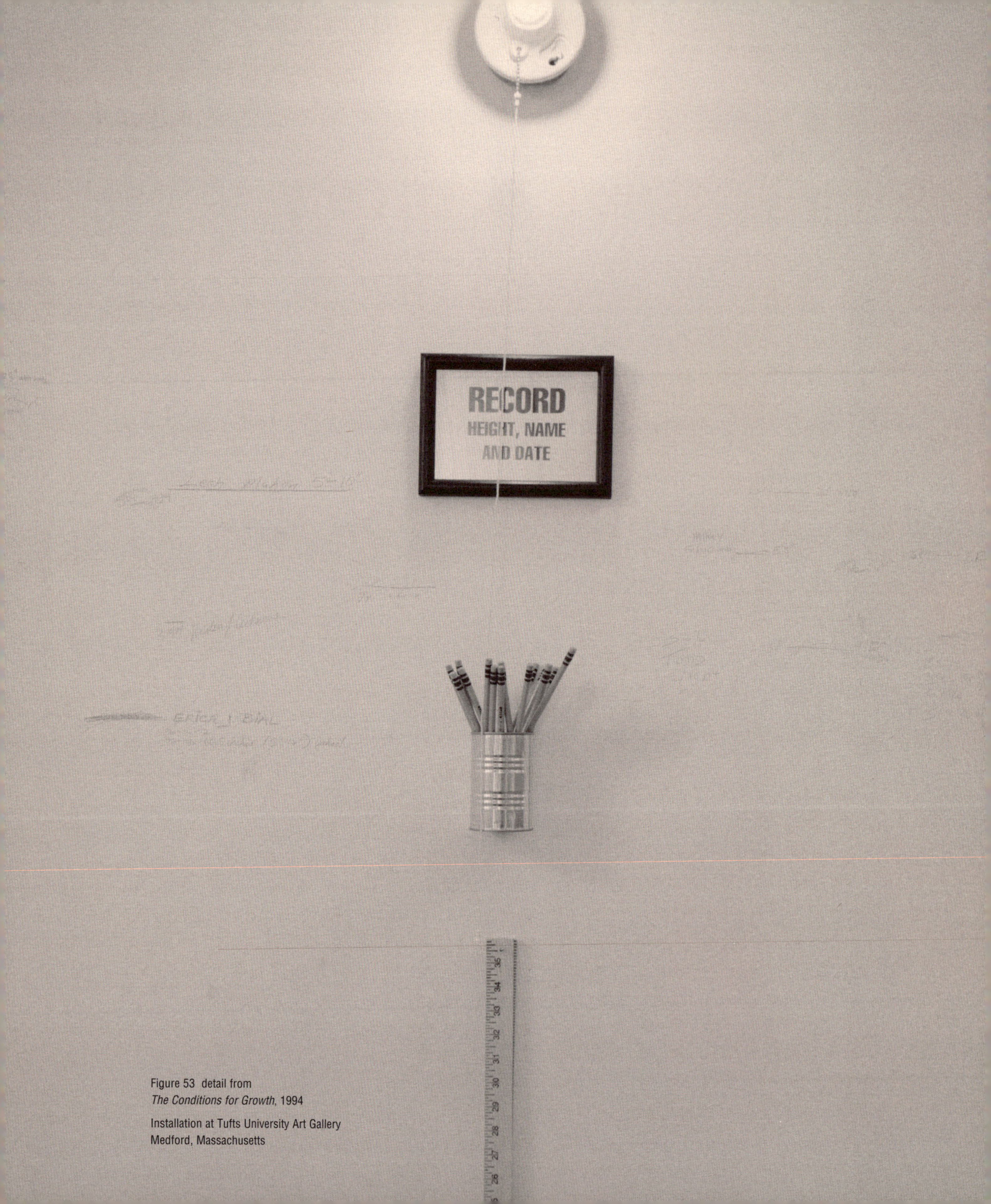

Figure 53 detail from
The Conditions for Growth, 1994

Installation at Tufts University Art Gallery
Medford, Massachusetts

Ellen Rothenberg

Born 1949
New York, New York

BFA '71, Cornell University
Ithaca, New York

MFA '78, Massachusetts
College of Art
Boston, Massachusetts

Lives and works in
Cambridge, Massachusetts

Selected Exhibitions

1994

The Conditions for Growth,
Tufts University Art Gallery
Medford, Massachusetts

Partial Index and *A Probability Bordering on Certainty*,
Portland Museum of Art
Portland, Maine

The Label Show: Contemporary Art and the Museum
Museum of Fine Arts
Boston, Massachusetts

Milena Diptova in Context
Institute of Contemporary Art
Boston, Massachusetts
catalogue

1993

Partial Index and selections from *A Probability...*,
Kent Gallery, New York, NY

Partial Index and *A Probability...*,
University Art Museum, UCSB
Santa Barbara, California
catalogue

An excerpt from The Anne Frank Project,
The Bunting Institute,
Radcliffe College
Cambridge, Massachusetts
catalogue

1992

Three Choices,
Barbara Krakow Gallery
Boston, Massachusetts

The Object is Bound,
Stephen Wirtz Gallery
San Francisco, California

1991

Boston Now,
Institute of Contemporary Art
Boston, Massachusetts

Center Margins,
Howard Yezerski Gallery
Boston, Massachusetts
catalogue

1990

Installation and Place,
Boston Center for the Arts
Boston, Massachusetts

1989

Reproductions,
Boston Museum of Fine Arts
Boston, Massachusetts

Allusion Dimension,
Rose Art Museum,
Brandeis University
Waltham, Massachusetts
catalogue

Explorations in Handmade Paper,
DeCordova Museum
Lincoln, Massachusetts
catalogue

Speak!,
Massachusetts College of Art
Boston, Massachusetts
catalogue

Alternative Mediums,
Monserrat College of Art
Beverly, Massachusetts

1988

Boston Now,
Institute of Contemporary Art
Boston, Massachusetts
catalogue

Fellowship Show,
Artists Foundation
Gallery/Cityplace
Boston, Massachusetts

1986

New Performance on Video,
New England Foundation for the Arts
Boston, Massachusetts

1976

Documents,
Boston Visual Artists Union
Boston, Massachusetts

1975

Eight Artists Recent Work,
Institute of Contemporary Art
Boston, Massachusetts

1974

Cayuga Exotica,
Johnson Museum of Art
Cornell University
Ithaca, New York

Selected Performances

1992

Hello Traitor...,
Festival Giannozzo,
Berlin, Germany

1988

Subway/Rebus, Artstops Program
Boston, Massachusetts

Common Sense, Cityplace
Boston, Massachusetts

Selected Performaces (continued)

1987

Common Sense,
Real Art Ways
Hartford, Connecticut

Speak!Speak!Speak!,
Real Art Ways
Hartford, Connecticut

5, collaboration with
Linda Fisher,
Sound Art, Mobius, Boston
Massachusetts

The Great Circle,
Artstops Program
Cambridge, Massachusetts

1986

Speak!Speak!Speak!,
Boston Film and Video Foundation
Boston, Massachusetts

1985

Every dog has its day,
Contemporary Arts Forum
Santa Barbara, California

1984

Episodes,
Mobius, Boston, Massachusetts

Soapbox,
Mobius, Boston, Massachusetts

Portrait,
Mobius, Boston, Massachusetts

1983

Outdoor Project,
Open Space Gallery
Victoria B.C., Canada

Mission of the Spies,
Boston Film and Video Foundation,
Boston, Massachusetts

1982

A bird, a monkey and a fish:
Who eat who and what?,
Boston Film and Video Foundation
Boston, Massachusetts

1981

She Wants . . .,
Massachusetts College of Art
Boston. Massachusetts

Man on the Street,
Boston Film and Video Foundation
Boston, Massachusetts

1980

She Wants. . .,
Johnson Museum of Art,
Cornell University
Ithaca, New York

Invitation,
Emerson College,
Boston, Massachusetts

She Wants. . .,
Boston City Hall,
Boston, Massachusetts

Visitor From the East,
Visible Light Gallery,
Santa Barbara, California

Lecture on Jackson Pollock,
Institute of Contemporary Art
Boston, Massachusetts

1979

16 x 18 x 25,
Franklin Furnace, New York NY

Big Performance,
Boston Film and Video Foundation
Boston, Massachusetts

1978

X Tape + Rock,
The Helen Shlien Gallery
Boston, Massachusetts

Duet Arts Festival
University of Massachusetts
Boston, Massachusetts

Ouroboros,
Punkt Data Gallery
Boston, Massachusetts

Selected Collections

Museum of Fine Arts,
Boston, Massachusetts

Rose Art Museum
Brandeis University
Waltham, Massachusetts

Charlene Engelhard
Concord, Massachusetts

Barbara Krakow, Krakow Gallery
Boston, Massachusetts

Kathryn Jane Gips
Boston, Massachusetts

Lucille and Rick Spagnuolo
Boston, Massachusetts

Selected Publications

Art News, 3/94
"Ellen Rothenberg," Mary Haus

The Village Voice, 1/18/94
"Voices, Choices," Kim Levin

Santa Barbara News Press, 12/31/93
"The Best of 1993," Michael Darling

Santa Barbara News Press, 10/8/93
"A Frank Diary," Michael Darling

Boston Globe, 6/23/93,
"A vital re-viewing of Anne Frank's Life," Christine Temin

Art New England, June/July 1993,
"Preview," Rachel Weiss

San Francisco Examiner, 4/24/92,
"Conceptual Art by the book," David Bonetti

Boston Globe, 10/15/92
"Galleries show their finest artists for fall," Nancy Stapen

Boston Phoenix, 5/31/91,
"Ideas 'R' us," Rebecca Nemser

Boston Globe, 5/29/91,
"Boston Now 10 unites potent works," Christine Temin

Boston Phoenix, 2/1/91, "On and Off The Street," Rebecca Nemser

Bay Windows, 1/17/91,
"The Politics of 'Getting In' "

Boston Globe, 1/10/91,
"Critics Tip," Christine Temin

Boston Globe, 1/9/91, "Marginalized People and Issues Take Center Stage at Yezerski Gallery," Christine Temin

Boston Sunday Globe, 12/30/90,
"Best of 1990," Christine Temin

Boston Phoenix, 12/28/90,
"Outstanding Art"

Art New England, 5/90,
"A Delicate Balance," Peter Walsh

Boston Globe, 5/3/90,
"Making room for artworks," Living/Arts, Christine Temin

Boston Phoenix, 5/4/90, "Places in the Heart," Rebecca Nemser

Boston Sunday Globe, 12/24/89,
"Best of 1989-Young Stars Decreasing Spaces," Christine Temin

Boston Sunday Globe, 12/3/89,
"Annual Lois Foster Exhibit at Brandeis is Rich and Evocative," Robert Taylor

Boston Sunday Globe, 11/19/89,
"Culture, Nature, Common Themes in Exhibit," Sandra Braverman

Boston Phoenix, 11/10/89, "Many Dimensions," Rebecca Nemser

Boston Globe, 10/03/89, "Paper Takes on New Dimensions," Christine Temin

Art New England, 5/89, "Ellen Rothenberg/Massachusetts College of Art," Kalo Clarke

Boston Globe, 4/16/89, "MFA...a refreshing sense of purpose," Robert Taylor

Boston Phoenix, 3/17/89, "20th Century Unlimited," David Bonetti

Boston Globe, 3/3/89, "The provocative art of Ellen Rothenberg," Christine Temin

Boston Phoenix ,7/1/88, "Paper Prophets"

The Boston Globe, 6/24/88, "The Paper Chase at the ICA," Christine Temin

Art New England, 3/88, "Aesthetics Without Answers," Marilyn Arsem

The Boston Globe Calendar, 2/26/87, "The T Gets On Track With Art," Ted Drozclowski

High Performance, Fall 1985, "Viewpoint," "Dog Days," Bill Anderson

Vanguard, "Locations, National," Volume 13, 2/84, Jane Young

Art New England, "New Genres, New Fellowships," Vol. 4, No. 10, 11/83, Johanna Branson

High Performance, Issue 20, Vol. 5, No. 4. 1983

High Performance, "Artist's Chronicle," Issue 17/18, Vol. 5. No. 1 Spring/Summer 1982

Boston Performance Artists Letter, Winter Issue, Vol.1. No.2, 1988 "Interview," Ron Wallace

Lectures and Panels

"Language, Image, Metaphor and the Arts,"
Massachusetts College of Art
Boston, Massachusetts, 1994

"Rosemarie Trockel and German Feminism,"
Institute of Contemporary Art
Boston, Massachusetts, 1991

"Beyond the Object: Working with Living Artists," panel discussion,
New England Museum Assoc.
Mystic, Connecticut, 1990

"The Work of Sophie Calle," gallery talk,
Institute of Contemporary Art
Boston, Massachusetts, 1990

"Threatening the First Amendment, Censorship and the Arts," panel discussion,
Brickbottom Studios
Somerville, Massachusetts, 1990

"Not Defining Performance Art," panel discussion, Mobius
Boston, Massachusetts, 1987

"On a History of Performance Art," lecture,
Institute of Contemporary Art
Boston, Massachusetts, 1981

Artist in Residence

1987

Real Art Ways
Hartford, Connecticut

1986

Boston Film and Video Foundation
Boston, Massachusetts

1980

Emerson College,
Center for Women in the Media and Performing Arts
Boston, Massachusetts

Nova Scotia College of Art and Design
Halifax N.S., Canada

1978-83

Massachusetts College of Art
Studio for Interrelated Media
Boston, Massachusetts

Visiting Artist

1994

University of Massachusetts
Dartmouth, Massachusetts

Worcester State College
Worcester, Massachusetts

1993

University of California,
Santa Barbara, California

1992

Yale University
School of Art and Architecture
New Haven, Connecticut

School of the Museum of Fine Arts
Boston, Massachusetts

1988

School of the Museum of Fine Arts
Boston, Massachusetts

1987

Wesleyan University
Middletown, Connecticut

Hartford Art School
West Hartford, Connecticut

Trinity College
Hartford, Connecticut

Monserrat College of Art
Beverly, Massachusetts

Massachusetts College of Art
Boston, Massachusetts

1980

Cornell University
Ithaca, New York

University of California at Santa Barbara
Santa Barbara, California

1979

Manhattanville College,
Purchase, New York

School of the Museum of Fine Arts
Boston, Massachusetts

Massachusetts Correctional Institution
Framingham, Massachusetts

1978

Douglas College,
Rutgers University
New Brunswick, New Jersey

Support for this publication was provided by the Tides Foundation with additional funds from the LEF Foundation; paper was generously provided by Domtar Specialty Fine Papers.

The Conditions for Growth, Ellen Rothenberg's installation at Tufts Art Gallery, was funded in part by the New England Foundation for the Arts, with additional support from the National Endowment for the Arts and the Massachusetts Cultural Council, a state agency.

Design:
Judy Kohn,
Kohn Cruikshank Inc.
Boston, Massachusetts

Photography:
Figures 32, and 37– 40
by Grace Moy;
Figure 45 by Sky Bergman;
all other photographs by
Bruce T. Martin
Cambridge, Massachusetts

Paper:
Domtar Specialty Fine Papers
Montreal, Stamford, Chicago

Printing:
Mercantile Printing Company
Worcester, Massachusetts

Binding:
J.S. Wesby and Sons
Worcester, Massachusetts

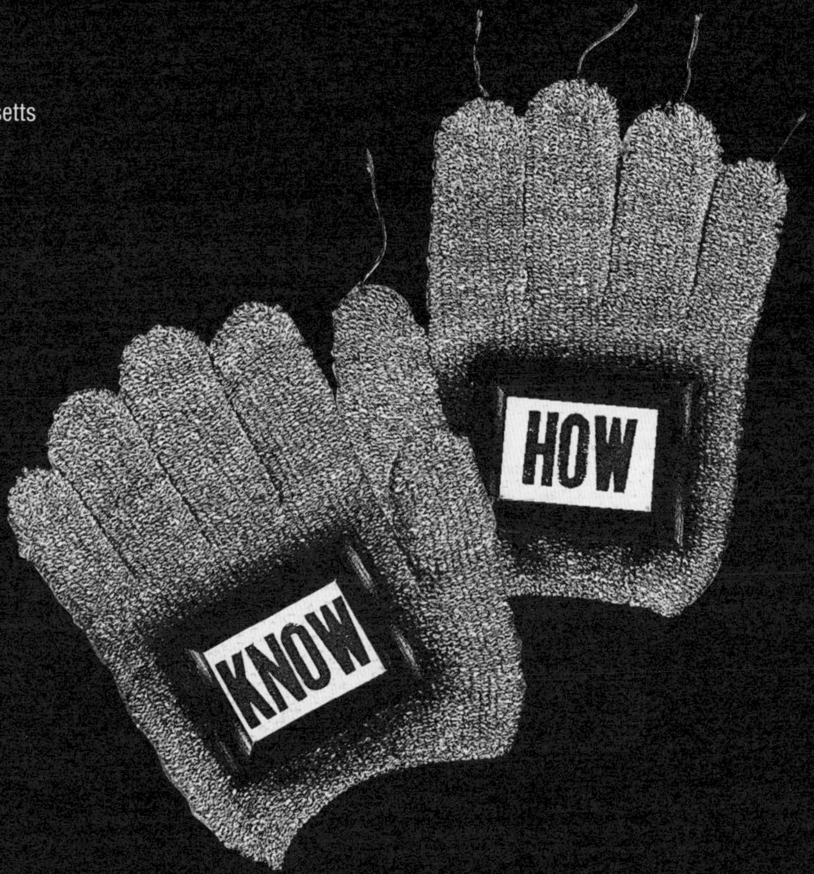